LLADRÓ

LLADRÓ

THE MAGIC WORLD OF PORCELAIN

SALVAT EDITORES, S.A.

Head of publication:
RICARDO MARTÍN

Publication Secretary:
JAIME VIÑALS

English version:
RICHARD LEWIS REE

Editorial Staff:
MIGUEL BARRACHINA
IGNACIO CUERVO
AMANCIO FERNÁNDEZ
PEDRO GONZÁLEZ

Photographs:
ENRIQUE CARRAZONI

Designer:
FERRAN JAVALOYES

© 1989 Salvat Editores, S. A.
Mallorca, 45-49
08029 Barcelona
ISBN: 84-345-4860-7
D.L.: B-18.670-1989
Printing: IHASA-1989
Printed in Spain

Collaborators

Lladró: Miracle, Magic, Myth:
JESÚS TORBADO

*Writer. Television and screenwriter. Author of travelogues and
numerous books and winner of several literary awards, including:
Alfaguara (1965), Planeta (1976), Mariano de Cavia (1982)
and Spanish Prize for Journalism.*

History of porcelain:
GEOFFREY A. GODDEN

*Fellow of the Royal Society of Arts,
Member of the British Antique Dealers' Association
and author of more than 20 books on porcelain, in particular*
Lowestoft Porcelains; Ridgway Porcelains; Godden's Guide
to Mason's China and other Ironstone Wares; The Encyclopaedia of British
Pottery and Porcelain Marks, *and* Staffordshire Porcelain.

Years that are history. The most recent history.
A future already present:
ROSENDO RAIMUNDO VERDAGUER

*Writer-publicist. Graduate in Philosophy and Letters.
Author of radio scripts on artistic and literary subjects
and of several books of narrative.*

Caprichos in porcelain:
MASAAKI MAEDA

*Professor of Western Ceramic Art at Department of Art History,
Musashino Art University, Tokyo. Author of many essays and papers
on Greek Art and European Ceramic Art, and of books
such as* Story of European Ceramics *and* Victoria & Albert Museum *(ed.).*

Contents

LLADRÓ: MIRACLE, MAGIC, MYTH

Juan, the eldest of the Lladró brothers, has the air of a dreamer; his grey eyes appear always to be looking beyond reality, as if there he might find the answer to the dilemma of his own existence. Perhaps for this reason he seems to be not much «realist», distant. If he were to abandon his elegant attire as president of the Administrative Council of Lladró Ltd, he could be taken for a gentle poet, or an absent-minded and dreamy painter, or a philosopher who always leaves the house without a penny in his pocket.

He has paid a mid-morning visit to the *Casa de los Artistas* (Artists Workshop), the most isolated, most advanced, and most secret building of the whole Lladró factory complex in Tavernes Blanques, a stone's throw away from the city of Valencia. The *Casa de los Artistas* is a haven of peace and industry within that other haven of peace and industry which is the Lladró factory, amongst the variety and bustle of the other industries in the area. A clear, diaphanous light and a cosy silence envelop the immense complex which, for many years, has been providing the world with a graceful form of beauty which very quickly acquired its own classicism. Rather than the usual kind of industry, it gives the impression of being a welcoming residence where people live happily together. The huge swimming pool in the central area of the complex, the other sporting facilities close by, the amazing garden-nursery at the top of the entrance structure, the dark building, modern yet totally unobtrusive, which is the nerve centre of the «Lladró city», and then the elegant white buildings inside which almost two thousand people daily produce marvellous porcelain pieces, the lushness of the grass, the unexpected cleanliness of this secret world; none of this allows the visitor to

Juan Lladró is the eldest of the three brothers, who together have ensured the extraordinary development of the celebrated porcelain pieces that bear their name. A great dreamer, his grey eyes seem capable always of perceiving what is new beyond the limits of reality.

imagine the mystery it contains and the myth which came into being here like a sacred fruit.

A girl, exhausted by her walk and the heat, tries, wide-eyed, to find the connection between the symbols on her plan and the buildings before her. She has undoubtedly come from far away, attracted by the myth which, now that she is faced with it, she cannot unravel. She has doubtlessly dreamt of discovering the sacred place where those objects she admires and loves so much are created; perhaps she has even dared to dream that she will meet one of their creators. And now Juan Lladró passes in front of her, stops to offer his help, and says that yes, those are indeed the Lladró workshops. She, in turn, says «thank you» and looks back with surprise at her map. Then she looks up again, undecided and confused, while Juan carries on towards his office, his turbulent and fertile mind probably shaping a new porcelain figure, yet to be realised: form, colour, expression, pose, nuance... just as he has always done and always will do.

He is not too fond of the word «miracle».

—But perhaps it is all a small miracle; yes —he says with an open smile—. We have undoubtedly been blessed by something. We are believers and maybe someone somewhere is watching over us. Undoubtedly a miracle is to be found here from the financial, business and commercial points of view; but that is not what I meant. The big question mark is to be found in porcelain itself.

José, the second eldest of the Lladró brothers, is a healthy, big, solid-looking man. His tasks as business organiser have yet to erase the lingering signs of many generations of Valencian market gardeners.

Vicente, the youngest, has big eyes and a deep and determined gaze. When he speaks, his delicate hands appear to model his words in the air. He shows hardly any traces of the little peasant boy he once was. Being the youngest, he had less contact with the land than his two elder brothers.

—Juan is the most modern of the three of us; he's the innovator —says Vicente—. José is more of a conservative, more classical. And I'm somewhere in between. Since we always take decisions by a majority of two, we always find the perfect balance. Maybe Juan wants to create new worlds out of nothing; José would rather keep the world the way it is, as long as he can purify it. I try to mediate between both passions, sometimes favouring one, sometimes the other. The result is always balance.

Such a balance is, perhaps, the result of that «collective art» which, when all is said and done, is exactly what Lladró porcelain is. A balance visible and tangible in every figure and every group; a balance which means harmony, the very essence of art. During the creative process the figures are like chess pieces in the hands of a lunatic. At times more than a hundred fragments lie, chrysalis-like, on the workbench, after they have been removed from the moulds: the hand of

José Lladró combines his special predilection for business with his passion for artistic creation within traditional confines. Both activities he carries out with his characteristic joviality and extroversion.

a ballerina, Don Quixote's nose, a dog's snout, a peasant-girl's basket, a Thai cap, the smiling eyes of a deer, a lover's melancholy face (...). All this hodgepodge, previously joined, designed and imagined by the artist, will once again find unity in the hands of the artisans, enamellers, painters, assemblers, etc. Hundreds of those who hold these porcelain fragments between their fingers, as if they were handling tiny fragile gods, at every stage of their production.

Where did all this splendour come from? How was it possible? Perhaps, when all is said and done, the true miracle lies in work and talent.

None of the three brothers is particularly interested in looking back on their laborious beginnings; their attitude is that everything was natural, spontaneous, measurable and foreseeable. Nevertheless, shining in the background we can see the names of their parents, of peasant-farmer stock: Juan Lladró Cortina, born in Almácera, and Rosa Dolz Pastor, native of the neighbouring village of Alboraya, who wished their children to have a better future than their own present. During the first third of this century, however, they were not even allowed to dream that their sons would be able to complete long, complicated courses of study. Quite simply, they could not afford them. Neither was their plot of land in Almácera, not far from where the great factory stands today, any guarantee of support for three male offspring.

—My mother —says Juan— wanted me to be a mechanic or a draughtsman, and eventually she went for the latter. But I couldn't just spend my time studying, so I started working at fifteen.

For four years Juan, the eldest, worked in the small chinaware section of the *Azulejera Valenciana* (Valencian Tileworks). During the Spanish war too many plates had been smashed and they had to be replaced with new ones. Juan started his working life as a decorator's apprentice, and José soon followed in his footsteps. Every afternoon, after work, they attended the Escuela de Artes y Oficios de San Carlos (School of Arts and Crafts) in Valencia. Their mother's original pragmatism was soon to become, for them, a firm vocation.

—Our mother always wanted us to follow a clean profession in which we wouldn't have to think too much. *Paint and sing*, she used to say. She had no idea how brilliant her idea was, though, because as a result of it all three of us were to follow the same path and eventually work together.

These three young brothers therefore followed each other's footsteps, constantly working, studying, and seeking perfection. At first apprentices and specialists in the *Azulejera Valenciana*, later professionals of repute in the Víctor de Nalda workshops, their desire to learn was insatiable. And every afternoon for seven years they attended classes by different masters in a corner of Europe which has traditionally been one of the richest breeding grounds

Vicente is the youngest of the Lladró brothers and has a special gift for modelling, both the material with which he gives life to his beautiful creations, and the balance of the company, essential to carry out all kinds of projects.

for arts and crafts. Juan and José felt more inclined towards painting; Vicente was to mark a slight change in direction through his preference for sculpture. As if guided by a mysterious hand, the Lladró brothers marked out the first steps towards that *collective art* so characteristic of their porcelain figures today. And first thing in the morning or last thing at night, in the midst of so much effort, they still found time to help their father cultivate the family market garden. Salaries during the difficult post-war years were modest in the extreme.

—We began working when we were still practically children and knew absolutely nothing —Juan recalls—. Tile decoration, study and our own personal tastes pushed us on, little by little, to what we were to achieve later. That was a modest, routine form of creation which you could hardly describe as stimulating, but it was an indispensable foundation stone for more ambitious works. No artist has ever become great without first learning, no one is born with all wisdom. As in any other activity, art must also be learnt, experimented with and repeated a thousand times to achieve maximum purity.

This individualised art, once they were outside the workshops where they earned their living, was born in the small court in their family home. The firms for whom the Lladró brothers worked could offer them no possibility to develop their innate talent: they wanted to create, produce their own work, and make a living from it. Juan and José began to sell their first pictures.

—I constantly tried out innumerable different kinds of painting materials. I painted a lot in the house of my fiancée, Carmen, who is now my wife, and once I did a portrait of one of her grandmothers, which she liked very much —José remembers.

—José and I painted everything: portraits, still lives, landscapes, but above all self-portraits because we ourselves were the cheapest models to hand. We began to sell our pictures, very cheaply of course. We've managed to recover a few of those early paintings, paying the earth for them, naturally.

Not only have they recovered paintings but also a few of their early ceramic and porcelain creations. In Vicente's office there is a vase, a solitary jewel which is classical yet very personal, on which each of the three young brothers has left his mark.

—I modelled it myself and my brothers decorated it. Then we sold it for just under a thousand pesetas. Many years later the buyer came to see us to say that he had that vase. We felt a special affection for it because it was one of the first truly artistic works we produced together. We insisted on buying it back and paid half a million pesetas for it. We would have paid what he asked and you can be sure that we wouldn't sell. It is a centrepiece of the thirty odd old Lladró works we have managed to recover, sometimes with great difficulty, for our museum-archive. Unfortunately porcelain is so fragile... In two years time all these pieces, together with a selection of others from different periods, will be presented in New York at the opening of the Lladró Museum.

The two-handled vase, with its lid in the form of a chubby child and the delicate portrait of an nineteenth-century lady on the body, stands on the topmost of a set of shelves alongside a bust of Don Juan Lladró, the father. He wears the typical cap of the *huertano* (Valencian market-gardener) and on his face stand out the determined set of the mouth and the intense gaze of solidarity that his sons have inherited from him. This bust is also one of Vicente's best sculptures and an indelible tribute to the man who pushed his three sons towards wider horizons. This realistic bust, an exact copy of the model, contrasts strongly with the baroque vase and the subtlety of certain classical Lladró pieces, stylised, ethereal figures which are miracles of imagination and sensitivity.

Around about this time a labour dispute which a contemporary observer would have considered trivial but which a prophet would have qualified as providential, caused the three brothers to give up their jobs with Nalda, the firm that had taken them on thanks to their industriousness and creative talents in the field of porcelain. Differences of opinion regarding wages convinced the Lladró brothers that the time had come to branch out on their own and follow the path that their imagination and sensitivity were already beginning to mark out for them. The year was 1953.

Several years previously, when they were still working at the *Azulejera*, they had set up a small kiln in the back yard of their house. Juan half closes his eyes as he remembers those difficult times.

—We had a small kiln at home, in the yard, and we began to work there, while our mother watched and encouraged us and our father gave us a hand with the small firewood kiln. That little kiln was the real birth of Lladró. We used to work hour after hour, day and night, finishing off our day by studying and working in the fields. We never stopped. We made copies of contemporary and classical figures, cornucopias, candelabra, graceful gazelles, earthenware flowers... Those flowers for decorating lamps became the fashion

The Artists' studio is the building within the Lladró complex in Tabernes Blanques where all the creative impulses of the company are born, nurtured and transformed into works.

very quickly and began to sell quite well, and we certainly needed to sell some of our work in order to keep going.

—Apart from those ceramic pieces —says José—, we now began to try out porcelain. It was very painstaking, delicate work and what we produced we sold at ridiculously low prices. There were pieces that took all three of us several days to make, with the help of our father, and which hardly brought in enough money to pay for our expenditure. We were well trained and experienced in all artistic fields, but there was no demand for our work. Sometimes I feel nostalgia for those hours spent painting delicately, one by one, the fingers of a ballerina that Vicente had spent hours

Vicente Lladró beside his own bust, which he himself modelled. In addition to his particular characteristics, the sculpture reflects the vigour and integrity of a race capable of making the maximum sacrifices in order to obtain a well-made work.

and hours modelling. Then came the interminable experiments with materials, with the temperature of the kiln that had been lent to us at first and hired out to us later; the never ending desire to advance, discover, improve. Commercial success eluded us, though, and we had many lean months. All we could sell were the earthenware flowers, ballerinas dressed up in tulle, pirouetting on one foot, and wrapped up in cellophane, and the occasional giraffe whose legs were so delicate that it seemed to be suspended in mid air. We never skimped for a moment since we knew that this was our real apprenticeship. What's more, those early works were genuine Lladró pieces.

If the time needed to produce those delicately worked figures had been justly valued, they would have had to be sold at astronomical prices. The Lladró brothers were happy just to sell them, at any price, as if they knew that they were passing through an experimental phase which would lead them on to greater things, an investment in time which would later result in a veritable empire in the world of porcelain. Between firings the three brothers joined their father to work the land, especially at night, when Don Juan arrived home from the metal workshop where he worked during the day. Both he and his wife had committed themselves to the struggle to achieve a brilliant future for their sons; and for this reason they decided to sell off a piece of their land so that they could carry on with their experiments.

Vicente Lladró with one of his collaborators, José Puche, examining the sketch for a piece.

The Lladró brothers intervene directly and constantly in all the different production phases. Here, José (left) and Juan (right) are with Julio Ruiz, head of decoration (centre), deciding on the finish for a number of pieces.

—In the end we lost the land and the money we had got for it —José recalls.

In the meantime, of course, they had become acquainted with porcelain, that elusive, mysterious queen of the very earth itself. Having come to know her, they would never abandon her.

—We used to collect broken, fireproof fragments from the *Altos Hornos* (Blast Furnaces) in Sagunto and pieces of brick from the sea shore. With these we began to build a true kiln. At first the neighbours complained about the smoke it gave off —we had it in our back yard— but at last we were able to reach the temperatures necessary to vitrify porcelain, even with that rudimentary, home-made kiln. We began to try out the techniques we were to apply later: systems of firing, temperatures, mixtures, tones. Porcelain is

In the obtention of Lladró porcelain pieces the hands, those marvellous instruments capable of transforming into reality everything that human thought can imagine, are of primordial importance, and their role extends from modelling to putting the most delicate finishing touches throughout the different production stages.

obviously the result of artistic processes, but it would be impossible to produce without the help of science and complex techniques. From the creative point of view, porcelain can be compared with the cinema, which is also simultaneously art, technique, and industry. If one of these elements lets you down, the result is failure. So not only did we have to listen to the call of our imagination and our sensitivity, but also to study technique in the strict sense of the word, the industrial side of porcelain, when it came to creating. Vicente continued to model, Juan and I drew designs and decorated; Juan and Vicente struggled with the kiln and chemistry; I did research into work itself, into our own work method. Together we searched for forms, expressions, tonalities, glosses. We tried to produce results that satisfied us before attempting to satisfy others.

In the meantime they tried to eke out a living through the sale of objects for which there was most demand: flowers, decorated plates, candelabra: fashionable pieces which they themselves sold in Valencia. But it was not enough. At one moment of deep pessimism they were about to go their separate ways; but they reckoned without their mother, who continually encouraged them to stay together.

—She had a mysterious power capable of channelling our lives without forcing us. She placed obstacles in our path, and offered incentives to make us strive towards what she considered the best

This view of the Porcelanas Lladró city shows the workshops (in the background) and part of the sports complex (foreground) in which all the members of the great family, formed by everyone who works for the company, carry out competitions and sporting activities.

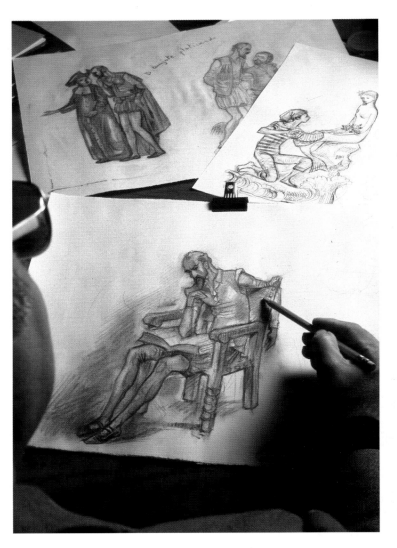

A figure is obtained first from an idea expressed in a drawing in which every detail which will later transform the idea into a work of art is accurately represented.

objective for us. And she certainly wasn't mistaken. Thanks to her support we finally decided to carry on together.

Juan was by now nearly thirty years old and still a bachelor. Every day he and his brothers would study, work the fields and nurture the impossible dream of starting their own factory. Their weekly earnings fell just short of two thousand pesetas, and with this they had to make do.

—We ourselves went to buy our varnishes in Manises, where the big ceramic works were, transport them to the railway station in a little cart, register it on the train, and then catch the *trenet*. Then we would repeat the process with the plaster we brought from Valencia. Those were hard times, it's true, but they were also fascinating times —says Vicente—. I don't know how many journeys I made between the ages of fifteen and twenty, loaded up to the limit of my strength.

Little by little a miracle was happening, with the same presence and perfection as that of a porcelain figure. Effort, enthusiasm, passion, sensitivity, talent: these were the ingredients which were being fired together in the kiln formed by those three spirits. Even when failure seemed imminent, for them it did not exist. As with Mark Twain's innocents, so these artists ignored the fact that theirs was an impossible dream; precisely for this reason, it became reality.

And as a result, the miracle became magic.

—I don't believe in sudden changes —says José—, and in our work there is a constant transformation. It progresses imperceptibly day by day. Only by contemplating our work after one, two, or five years do we realise how it has developed. Style is not a fleeting flash of inspiration but the perfection produced by daily work. That's why in all our pieces you can see a continued style, the collective art of three people committed, heart and soul, to years of work in order to do something well.

They examined and researched everything, activities they began on the journeys they made when still young students —rewards for the good marks they obtained— to Madrid, Barcelona, and Zaragoza. They absorbed beauty and continually sought harmony, for harmony is the law of the gods. Juan recalls the days when they talked non-stop about Sèvres, Capodimonte, Buen Retiro, Meissen, Limoges: names which for them had magical connotations. Painters, alchemists, sculptors, poets, magicians, had all kept a thousand-year-long rendez-vous to produce what Marco Polo had called *porcellana*.

The foundations for the first factory were laid in 1958, when the Lladró brothers were now sure of what they were capable, when their knowledge of porcelain had reached the required level, and when they were finally sure that their works appealed to the sensitivity of others.

—Naturally —Juan assures us—, you can't make

Flowers are one of the complements that have most contributed to create the idea of perfection in Lladró pieces. Their highly difficult execution is entrusted to expert hands.

the same porcelain today that was produced in the past. Chinese vases contained natural kaolin and their transparency reminds us a little of the taste of home-baked bread. It can't be repeated. It can't be repeated because now it's impossible to fire the same piece seven times over, and smash hundreds of rejects until you achieve the piece you want. The wealth of princes couldn't finance such a project. Labour costs were very low in those days and extra expenses were minimal. Nevertheless, even the Chinese didn't manage to achieve the kind of technical perfection that we have. How can you get such delicacy with only one firing? Our forefathers would never have dreamt of such a possibility. And yet we're gradually achieving it.

The Lladró brothers have given to the world of porcelain a unique style and unmistakable forms, on the one hand, and numerous innovative techniques on the other. They have created a school. But what lies behind this style which is famous all the world over?

—Poetry, sensitivity, expressivity, harmony. We have managed to make what is difficult look easy. Each one of the pieces, although several people have intervened in its creation, seems to have been completed by one person only; and even though it's necessary to turn to technical processes, because otherwise the pieces would be too expensive —impossible, in fact— to produce, our porcelain is actually hand-made in every detail. The tonalities, so

difficult to achieve, have been reached after many experiments and trials. High temperatures tend to obliterate colours and our struggle has been to raise the tones during the single firing the figures undergo. The process of creating each figure is very laborious and extremely costly. *The Coach*, to take just one example, was produced after a whole year of study and preparation. Therefore our techniques not only allow us to produce works as perfect as those of two centuries ago, but also —and this fills us with pride because it is extremely important— to keep them within reach of ordinary people. It is no longer only kings and princes who can enjoy these exquisite objects; anyone can buy and admire them. This, I think, is worth emphasizing from the sociological point of view.

The piece reproduced here is entitled the "Coiffure" and it is one of the greatest contributions of Lladró porcelain to artistic creation. Indeed, it contains the elongation and stylisation of the forms of the girls, perfection in details (the hands and flowers) and the colour shade quality.

However, it is by no means easy that an object moulded from clay by a man's hands should be liked equally in Lapland and South Africa, in Singapore and Canada, in Spain and Australia, in the United States and Japan.

—Perhaps this is because our figures speak a universal language: they say something and this something is intelligible to any sensitive soul. They express our way of being and of seeing life. Of course we poeticise reality; we idealise it and turn our backs on pathos and violent dramatics. This is poetry and poetry is the most universal of all languages.

José speaks of delicacy, of the sensitivity each piece exudes, of its elegance. He also points out the necessary fact that all these spiritual elements should be «manufacturable». Ideas and imagination should be given form in stone: one must design, model, make moulds, join the parts, paint, apply the varnishes, bake. We come back to that magic moment when art and technique meet and support each other, like two loving parents who give birth to a wonderful child.

—Hardly anyone decorates *bajo cubierta* (below deck); that is, paints the figures before applying the enamel, that vitreous material that crystallises at high temperatures. It's a technique which is very difficult to master when the kiln is at full blast, and we're proud to have managed it. The colours of Lladró porcelain, which define and distinguish it, are the result of this technique.

And always the delicate and painstaking attention to perfection. Each figure is minutely studied and those that have a hair-line crack, a slight stain or any blemish, however small, are rejected.

—They tell us that we're working for a better world, and it's true —Vicente assures us—. Each porcelain figure is also a reflection of the spirit of its owner, because each figure is a hymn to beauty, to goodness, in a word, to love. This is the ultimate meaning of all our efforts.

Constantly faced with this endless obsession with marrying art and technology, the Lladró brothers found a hallmark for their works: they resorted to those elements with which they are so familiar, Nature and Chemistry.

This happened later, of course. At first they personally signed their works one by one. But when the «Lladró myth» began to spread all over the world and their figures were sought after everywhere, this operation took up too much time. So they found a hallmark. Thus while the craftsmanlike creative processes remained intact, the three great creative artists were spared such a routine task.

—We went back to the idea that has always guided us —says Juan Lladró—. Our porcelain pieces are works of art expressed through a highly perfected technique. So we looked for our symbol in Nature and Chemistry, the essential science in the art of porcelain. And we chose a flower, a flower in its purest simplicity.

This flower seller piece sets off the modesty and simplicity of the girl against the challenge involved in the flowers themselves, each one of which had to be made petal by petal.

A flower resting on an alchemical symbol whose meaning was lost a long time ago. It has become a timeless symbol that expresses man's efforts to master material and achieve beauty.

Under this symbol the Lladró brothers have transmitted the best of their inner selves all over the world. The delicacy of the pieces, which unites them in a common bond, seems to herald the coming of a better world. Their mysterious charm is a tangible metalanguage. The figures, so prodigiously varied, are a kind of apostolate of beauty, a means of communication between those who share a similar concept of man's life on earth.

—We don't set out to beautify reality —states Juan—, but rather to separate from reality everything that obscures its very soul, the vision of its very soul.

This is the final purpose, the «magic of Lladró art», which can be seen in groups such as *The Deer Hunt*, *The Three Wise Men* (a piece which the Pope has in his private rooms), the group of horses in the possession of Ronald Reagan, the pieces that belong to the Spanish Royal Family and other personalities the whole world over. *The Landau, The Coach, The Angel with Mandoline*; unforgettable pieces that over thirty-five years, lovingly conceived, designed, modelled, painted, varnished, and delivered to the fire of purification and perfection, have been given birth by the hands of the Lladró brothers.

It is hardly surprising, then, that those sensitive

The second Lladró generation consists of ten youngsters, some of whom are still children, most of whom will continue along the vigorous path begun by their fathers in the art of porcelain. On the previous page: Juan Vicente Lladró, Vicente's son, who is studying architecture; on this page: Rosa, the daughter of Juan Lladró (left), who studied Fine Arts, and Mari Carmen, the daughter of José (right), with a degree in managerial studies, already form the vanguard at the head of the company.

people who admire and possess these pieces should
have turned the three founders of the Lladró empire
into genuine living myths. Like this girl today who, in
the early hours of the morning, follows her plan in
search of one of the creators of the works she loves so
much, or at least the place where they are created.

They are like three strict yet imaginative judges
who day after day, hardly allowing themselves
holidays, analyse, study, and work on each piece, from
the initial processes at the *Casa de los Artistas* to the
final check before sending their figures to all four
corners of the globe.

José smiles with a mixture of satisfaction and
disquiet. He knows that his family surname is one of
the most well-known Spanish names all the world over.

—Sometimes our customers and friends put us in
an extremely awkward position. To be honest I feel
that all of us who possess Lladró figures are part of a
big family, not only all those people who dedicate their
lives to bring them into being... Anyway, as I was
saying, sometimes at exhibitions people come up to us
and show us their children's drawings and ask if we
think there's any chance of their becoming artists;
as if we were prophets! Then they try and have their
photographs taken alongside us or ask for our
autographs!

The second Lladró generation has already begun
to work in porcelain. One each of the brothers' children
forms part of the board of directors: Rosa, Juan's

The three Lladró brothers are aware that they form the centre of a myth charged with legends that have built up around them, and they are reconciled to carrying out this role since they consider it inherent in the nature of those artists who have managed to form a school.

daughter, who studied fine arts; Mari Carmen, a business studies graduate and José's daughter; and Juan Vicente, who studied architecture, Vicente's son. They are all twenty-six years old and will doubtless follow the same rigorous path as the three Lladró brothers, who managed to stay together and create together. The second Lladró generation is composed of ten children, some of them still very small and many of whom will undoubtedly follow in their fathers' footsteps. They have already absorbed that industrious, creative spirit that has urged their fathers on throughout their lives.

—Life passes by but art remains —says Vicente, paraphrasing the old Latin saying—. For this reason I believe that Lladró is much more important than me since it is the work of so many people giving of their best. It would be extremely selfish of me to sacrifice the firm for my own, personal profit, so I would feel extremely grieved if my children didn't carry on this tradition. It's a marvellous experience to be on a plane in a distant country and see that someone there knows the name Lladró; not because they know me as a person but because they know my work. And if they manage to identify it with my person, they receive me as someone who has beautified their lives. I live where I was born and I feel very proud to be Spanish and that my Spanish surname should be associated with the unique art form that is our porcelain.

Thus the «Lladró myth» has been forming; a myth

which, naturally enough, has begun to be charged with legends. The three brothers resignedly accept the magic of their name, like every artist who has created a school: it is inevitable.

Their plans for the future now are exactly the same as the plans they made for it in the past: to progress both creatively and technologically and to make a qualitative jump ahead so that their porcelains will become even more valuable, genuine exclusive gems, always counting on the support of their children, of the second generation, and of an invaluable human team who combine the technical skill and pride in their work necessary to enable the Lladró brothers to produce their works. This team is drawn mainly from neighbouring towns and villages and is formed mostly by women. The firm has, besides, achieved considerable prestige with its own training schools for painters. One of the classic problems of porcelain has always been to make it «workable»: the Tavernes Blanques team has always managed and continues to manage to «carry out» the ideas of the creators. With their collaboration and within that delicate and harmonious balance imposed by the different characters of the three brothers, little by little Lladró porcelain will increase its prestige, its distinction, and that message of love of life and of our fellow beings it has been transmitting for thirty-five years.

—My dream —says Vicente— is to leave a few pieces behind for posterity, a few pieces which anyone, on contemplating them, would be able unhesitatingly to say, «That's a Lladró». That would be enough.

Like the person who says, «This is an El Greco, a Michaelangelo, a Velázquez, a Rembrandt, a Picasso». The three brothers know full well that the new generation still has a lot of ground to cover but they are also sure that this ground will be cultivated so that the particular style which was so difficult to achieve will never perish. The «new art» which was born miraculously from the efforts of three Valencian peasant-farmers, the «collective art» with which each of the workers they themselves personally chose and trained feels a true identification, continues ceaselessly to progress towards perfection.

At the time of going to press, the limited-series pieces that have sold out have undergone a dramatic increase in value. This fact has led the three brothers to found, on the one hand, the Collectors' Society, which at the moment functions in the United States and Canada, and to create, soon, a Lladró museum in New York which would house the most representative examples of their art.

In the meantime Lladró will continue to create beauty and grace of increasing refinement and precision. And the three brothers —three individuals joined together in a single spirit— will continue their magic apostolate of offering a synthesis of love for beauty and goodness through the art of porcelain.

The three initial representatives of the second Lladró generation form a team which, having acquired a new tradition in the art of porcelain, will be able to cultivate it without losing anything of the already established style.

HISTORY OF PORCELAIN

Porcelain is the most beautiful of plastics. It is the most delicate and attractive of all man-made materials. I write of porcelain as a plastic and a man-made material although, of course, it is formed of a mixture of natural clays, earths or substances fused together at great heat to form a completely new material —one that will never revert to its origins or decay—. The ultimate body beautiful!

There are several types of porcelain which I will be discussing but let us first confine our attention to true porcelain (or hard-paste porcelain as it is sometimes called). This material comprises in simple terms china clay and china stone which are also known as *kaolin* (aluminium silicate) and *petuntse* (aluminium and potassium silicate). These are the all-important basic ingredients which, like flesh and bones, are dependent upon one another for success. Both are needed for only a combination of the two can produce true porcelain. Porcelain, when not specially tinted, possesses a fine white body which when fired at the correct temperature is translucent, at least in its thinnest parts, and which when of a suitable form will "ring" like a bell —this last is the Oriental test for porcelain rather than the translucency which the Europeans find so desirable—.

The basic raw materials, including decomposed granite, are not necessarily all that pure and important trace elements can find their way into the mix —perhaps simply from the water used to dampen or liquefy the mix so that it can be thrown on the potter's wheel or poured into moulds—. A typical analysis of an example of eighteenth century Chinese porcelain would give the following approximate result:

Silica (SiO$_2$)	70,2 %
Alumina (Al$_2$O$_3$)	24,2 %
Potash (K$_2$O)	3,1 %
Lime (CaO)	1,4 %

plus traces of soda, magnesia, lead oxide and iron oxide.

This table of percentages will not be constant over all eighteenth century Chinese porcelains for, although the Oriental mix is remarkably constant, slight differences will occur. Incidently, this father and mother of all later porcelains is extremely similar to the fine porcelain body used to produce the modern Spanish *Lladró* masterpieces.

It is right that I should begin by quoting the makeup of Chinese porcelain because the Chinese were the first to produce porcelain, probably well over a thousand years ago. We do not know the exact date of its introduction even to a hundred or perhaps even to a thousand years! It was also introduced rather than invented, for its successful development would have been a gradual progression from the manufacture of simple earthenwares and stonewares.

Firstly, the correct ingredients –the *kaolin* and *petuntse* (china clay and china stone) or ingredients very close to these– would have to be located and used by the potters. The materials are quite rare and occur in workable quantities only in certain parts of the world. Next the difficult high temperature firing techniques would have to be mastered. Even an ideal porcelain mix will not be translucent if under-fired; while, if over-fired, the object will melt into a shapeless blob. It is the high-firing of the porcelain

The art of porcelain is something of such perfection that, despite the centuries that have passed since its discovery, it still demands the strictest observance of regulations and proportions in mixing and in the combination of the different ingredients from which it is produced.

mix, at some 1.450° centigrade, which distinguishes this body. Further developments involved the perfection of a suitable covering glaze, one that enhanced rather than marred the basic porcelain form. A true hard-paste porcelain such as the Chinese perfected is vitrified in the firing and is therefore watertight even without any covering glaze, although this added glass-like covering does make the otherwise rough surface more attractive, even sensual, and gives a much improved surface for decoration.

It is relevant to note that the standard method of production employed by the Chinese was to fire the porcelain once, not twice as was the case with most later Continental manufacturers. On the Continent of Europe it was the practice to fire the porcelain at a low heat, then to glaze the object and finally re-fire at a temperature in the approximate range 1.350° to 1.450° centigrade. The Oriental porcelains were fired body and glaze together in a single firing. With the later, mainly English, soft-paste mixes the wares were submitted to their highest firing before glazing –a reversal of the Continental technique–. Obviously in all cases any over-glaze decoration –enamel colours or gilding– was matured and fixed at lower temperature firings.

The Chinese gradually perfected their porcelains and their ceramics (earthenwares and stonewares as well as porcelain) began to find their way across the world. The now famous Venetian traveller and merchant, Marco Polo, on his return from China at the end of the thirteenth century wrote in glowing terms of the Chinese porcelains although the first printed account of his adventures did not appear in Europe until 1477. Reputedly, Marco Polo was the first to use a version of the term porcelain when he likened the

white luxurious surface to that of the beautiful cowrie shells which in Italy were called *porcellètta*. In England the most usual term was *china ware* (often abbreviated to china) meaning ware from China. The dealers in such goods were known as "chinamen" in the seventeenth and eighteenth centuries.

Chinaware or porcelain found its way in small quantities into the Near East and into Europe from at least the fourteenth century. At that time it was considered a great rarity and was extremely highly prized. Its possession was very much restricted to the heads of states, the nobles and the ultrarich. It was often mounted in gold or other metals and treated like a rare jewel.

The flow of Chinese porcelain into Europe on a commercial scale gathered momentum in the late sixteenth century at a time when the Portuguese still held a monopoly in the trade. This trade escalated with the capture by the Dutch of some Portuguese vessels which were carrying Chinese porcelains. Their cargoes when sold by the Dutch aroused great excitement and obtained high prices. The cargo of the Portuguese carrack (trading vessel) the *San Jago* was auctioned in Holland in 1602 and a further sixty tons of porcelain from the *Catarina* in 1604. These Chinese porcelains brought to Europe by the Portuguese were in the main useful articles intended for use on the table, comprising plates, dishes, bowls, small bowls and saucers and the like. In the main these porcelains were painted in underglaze-blue and were still often called "kraak", a term deriving from the Portuguese carracks in which the wares were carried to Europe.

The earliest European oil painting to depict such porcelain is probably that dated 1611 by N. Gillis and this banquet subject painting includes three Chinese blue and white dishes containing various fruits. At this period several European nations were striving to enter the trade to and from the East and various trading companies were set up. These were generally known as East India Companies for the trade was not restricted to China and Japan but covered a large area and embraced a wide range of commodities, of which porcelain formed only a minor part. It was, however, a vital constituent of the homeward cargo for, being heavy and watertight, it proved a helpful form of ballast making the vessel "sailworthy", to use the contemporary term.

The Dutch East India Company early in the seventeenth century sought to monopolise the trade with China and Japan. These nations placed many obstacles in the way of the Europeans and much of the trade was carried on not direct with these countries but via other foreign ports to which the Chinese shipped their goods. Nevertheless, the Dutch Company's vessel, the *Gelderland*, in 1614 brought home to Holland nearly seventy thousand pieces of Oriental porcelain.

From about this time the Dutch traders began to order special shapes and patterns better suited to the growing European market than some of the traditional Eastern forms. After Oliver Cromwell's treaty with King John IV of Portugal in 1654 the English were enabled to trade more freely in the South Seas. Their main station was Bantam, from where vessels were sent to the Chinese port of Amoy where they were able to purchase Japanese as well as Chinese wares. Full details of the development of this Anglo-Chinese trade, later centred on Canton, are given in Geoffrey Godden's specialist book *Oriental Export Market Porcelain* (Granada Publishing, London, 1979). The

importation of Chinese and to a lesser extent Japanese porcelains into Europe in the eighteenth century was truly vast, amounting to millions of pieces. It is perhaps relevant to mention that the imports comprised two basic types. Firstly, the bulk commercial importations of the various European East India Companies. These comprised in the main long runs of useful objects of standard forms decorated in a few popular patterns. Secondly, there were the "Private Trade" importations. These comprised smaller purchases of a more individual nature and were the domain of the ship's captain, the "Supra-cargo" and the crew. The individual designs, for example the armorial decorated porcelains, were "Private Trade" imports and were not covered by the bulk imports of the very large trading companies.

It was these novel decorative and useful white-bodied Chinese (and Japanese) porcelains that stirred European potters, as well as Kings and Emperors, to try to produce comparable objects and so establish such a desirable industry in their own land rather than be dependent on supplies that had to be shipped across thousands of miles of unfriendly seas.

The problem was to find the basic raw materials or their equivalent –the *Kaolin* and *Petuntse* of the Chinese or the China Clay and the China Stone–. Until these were found, the potters could only seek to purify and whiten their Earthenwares and Stonewares. One relatively easy way partly to achieve the desired effect was to coat the surface of the clay-coloured earthenware with a thin wash or coating of a whitened glaze. This glaze or slip was usually made white and opaque with oxide of tin. These so-called tin-glazed earthenwares include generic types such as Delft, Maiolica or Faience, designations used to distinguish such tin-glazed earthenwares produced in different parts of Europe and the Near East.

Particularly in Holland, France and the British Isles such Delft and Faience wares were decorated very much in the style of the Oriental porcelains, the blue and white designs being the most popular as well as the easiest to produce. Decorative as these tin-glazed earthenwares were, they could not compete in use with the imported Oriental porcelains. They were more clumsily potted and, although thicker in gauge, were less durable than the thinly potted porcelains. The body was prone to breakage and cracking and the white covering glaze was very liable to flaking especially at the edges.

Importantly, the tin-glazed earthenwares did not prove suitable for the fashionable habit of drinking tea (or indeed for coffee or chocolate). The Chinese

White porcelain Chinese figure from the XVI-XVIIth-century and Fukien province (National Museum of Oriental Art, Rome). While other Chinese ceramists produced coloured porcelain, those from this region always worked with a kind of white porcelain with which they created statuettes above all. They are usually religious pieces and both their modelling and glazing border on perfection.

teawares were the ultimate and fashionable society could not be seen without their Chinese porcelain "tea equipage".

Later in this book we will be very much concerned with decorative and finely modelled figures and groups. These were, in general terms, a later European development. The main imports of Oriental porcelains were useful wares –tablewares and sets of large vases–. This is not to say that the Chinese and Japanese potters in the late seventeenth and early eighteenth centuries did not produce figure and animal models but these tended to be somewhat crudely potted (to European eyes) and were popular for their novelty rather than for their excellence of modelling.

There is one general class of Chinese porcelain figures which may perhaps be compared with the later European figures. I here refer to the *Blanc de Chine* porcelains, to use the generic French term for the white and undecorated porcelains made at or near Tê Hua (Dehua) in the Province of Fukien (Fujian) rather than at Ching-tê-Chên (Jingdezhen), the great inland centre of the porcelain industry in China. These white porcelains can in modelling and sharpness of potting be quite beautiful. Their success depends on the purity of the body and the glaze and on the skill of the modeller and the potter –or rather on the skill of the whole production team, to use modern terms–. It is a matter of wonderment that such perfect objects could have been produced in conditions that today would be considered primitive. Wood-firing in tunnel-like kilns rising up a hillock with no method of controlling the temperature –only centuries of expertise!–.

In an effort to emulate the Oriental porcelains various European potters tried adding glass to pottery mixes in the hope that this might result in the sought-after translucency. Needless to say, the addition of glass caused difficulties in the firing and the objects tended to collapse. Other early problems arose from the smoke, if not flame, in the kiln which caused staining and discolouration of the objects being fired. To overcome this, the later and more successful wares were fired in *saggers,* or protective fire-clay boxes, which enabled the objects to be cooked (!) but not burnt.

Perhaps the earliest reasonably successful effort to produce a white-bodied type of porcelain in Europe was attempted in Florence in about 1575. These so-called Medici porcelains are of the soft-paste variety, that is they are an artificial porcelain, in this case made up of a local impure kaolin, sand, lime, rock crystal and glass. These now extremely rare Italian mock-porcelains are true museum pieces. They are remarkable for not seeking to copy Oriental forms or styles of decoration: it was the basic near magical body that was esteemed.

The sophisticated and successful French were also seeking to introduce their own porcelain industry. In the latter part of the seventeenth century experiments were being conducted in Rouen and at St Cloud, although the products of both centres were artificial or soft-paste porcelains fired at a relatively low temperature.

The first experiments to produce true or hard-paste porcelain in Europe were centered in Germany, or to be more exact in Saxony, where, prompted by the all-powerful Augustus the Strong (an early and omnivorous collector of Oriental porcelains), Ehrenfried Walther von Tschirnhaus (d. 1708) and Johann Friedrich Böttger (d. 1719) succeeded in producing a hard stoneware that could be polished like

a gem. This attractive class of ceramic led to the white-bodied pieces at first formed from Colditz clay and calcified alabaster.

By about 1710 more suitable clays, or rather sources of kaolin, had been discovered and the quality of the new wares soon began to approach that of the true Chinese porcelain.

By 1710 a new enlarged factory had been established at Meissen in the old Albrechtsburg fortress. Their first essays were offered at the 1710 Leipzig Easter Fair but these first products of the factory did not find the expected ready sale. Augustus the Strong subsequently ordered J. J. Irminger, the Court Goldsmith, to design new forms for the tentative new works with its largely unskilled workforce, and from that point onwards the German porcelain industry sprang into life. It is interesting that the novel German wares of the 1710 period were not readily marketable although this can be explained by the fact that then, as now, the ability to produce a workable

"The Florist", a porcelain piece from towards 1748 (Museo degli Argenti, Florence) produced in Meissen, Saxony. It was in this German region that, for the first time in Europe, a porcelain was obtained that was comparable to that from the Orient. The grace of its figurines is characteristic of the rococo movement.

The firing of porcelain pieces is the culminating operation in all manufacturing processes. For this they are arranged in the kiln in such a way that they do not touch; the heat of the fire will do the rest. Previously, however, experience and technical knowledge will have ensured the quality of the pastes and studied their reactions to the effects of heat.

white porcelain is only the beginning of the struggle. You must be capable of fashioning it into pleasing objects or ornaments that will catch the public's fancy and which they will wish to purchase to adorn their homes. It is the happy marriage of the porcelain body with the creative skill of the designers and the talents of the workforce that create a saleable finished product.

This is not an appropriate place to detail the success of the Meissen factory or of the later related Dresden porcelains, but it is perhaps relevant to note that the Works enjoyed State support and patronage. The Meissen management were therefore not dependent on the sale of ordinary useful wares, such as blue-painted humble tea services, as were so many other early factories, particularly in England. The German factory could concentrate on the production of richly-decorated up-market wares, ornamental figures and groups, ornamental vases, life-size animal models and the like-prestige articles for the Emperor and his friends. Even in these circumstances some middle-market porcelains were produced, much of the added decoration being in the style of the fashionable Japanese and Chinese imports, in which connection the factory staff had the advantage of access to the world's largest collection of Oriental porcelain —that of Augustus the Strong himself—.

In spite of the strictly enforced security measures at the Meissen factory, the secret of porcelain making soon spread and small rival works were established at Vienna in about 1718 and shortly afterwards at Venice. The Nymphenburg factory in Bavaria is of especial interest in this study for the world-famous so gracefully posed figures of contemporary life, modelled by Franz Anton Bustelli, could be likened to

Porcelain from Nymphenburg, in Bavaria, modelled by Franz Anton Bustelli, the most famous of the artists who worked in the said manufactory in the XVIIIth century. His rococo works had nothing to do with oriental models. By virtue of the variety of types and elegance of its forms, this porcelain is comparable to that of Lladró, both having achieved a classical elegance.

the present-day Lladró models. Lovers of antique porcelains may possibly shudder at this comparison, but the products of both factories are classics. One represents eighteenth century skill and elegance and is priced in many thousands of pounds. The other represents modern excellence and is freely available at a fraction of the price of the older. Put a dozen examples of each type in a modern china store, priced in equal terms, and I am sure the average buyer seeking beauty and charm rather than age or rarity will choose the modern pieces.

Moving into France, we have the Vincennes and Sèvres factories which were in much the same financial position as Meissen and Dresden in Germany. Both enjoyed State support and both were consequently able to concentrate on the production of elaborately decorated costly articles. Vincennes and later Sèvres porcelains were however even less inspired by Oriental styles or shapes than their German counterparts. Instead new curved rococo styles were introduced as were rich and decorative ground colours. Again, like the Meissen porcelains, the more lavish articles were intended for Royal palaces and as Royal gifts and opulence of form, colour and gilding was the order of the day.

In complete contrast to this lavishness, there was a class of figures and groups which were very well and professionally modelled but which lacked added surface decoration or indeed even glaze. These *bisquit* porcelain figures are delightful, but alas rare, and they may be likened to the Oriental *Blanc de Chine* models insofar as both rely on the art of the sculptor —as do some modern Lladró models which are left in the white state—.

The early Vincennes porcelains and the post-1752 Sèvres wares (for the Works were moved to larger and more suitable premises in that year) were not like the Chinese or the Meissen porcelains but were of the soft-paste variety or *Pâte Tendre* as they would be termed in France. The combination of this soft-paste porcelain and the related glassy glaze helped to make the products of the factory particularly attractive as the added enamel colours tended partly to sink into the glaze and become part of it. Rich as the Sèvres porcelains undoubtedly are they have a pleasing mellowness.

However, by about 1772, soon after deposits of kaolin or china clay were found near Limoges, the Sèvres factory changed their standard mix and produced hard-paste porcelain, or *Pâte Dure*, which the factory termed "Porcelaine Royale". The new wares may well be technically more perfect than the earlier examples and the new body was certainly less troublesome in the firing, but the resultant hard-paste porcelains are rather too slick and cold for most collectors' tastes.

The discovery of kaolin at Limoges was, however, of inestimable importance to that locality as the pure deposits were to attract a host of porcelain manufacturers, many of whom still remain there and are of international repute. The Limoges kaolin was also shipped to other centres, notably to Paris where several very high class porcelain factories as well as decorating establishments were to be set up. The various Paris porcelains of the approximate period 1780-1820 represent a highwater mark for technical excellence and superb decoration in the French Empire style.

There were in Germany as well as in France many other smaller factories, but the Meissen (or Dresden)

Porcelain dairymaid from Sèvres (Museo degli Argenti, Florence), From Germany, the French manufactories were set up in Vincennes and Sèvres. Due to the lack of kaolin, the Sèvres factory produced so-called soft paste until around 1722 when, with the discovery of the said material, hard paste could be produced.

Vincennes porcelain jar and washbasin from around 1754-1756 (Museo degli Argenti, Florence). Although the Vincennes factory, like that of Sèvres, received state aid, it could not survive and in 1756 it merged with the Sèvres manufactory bringing with it almost all its methods, decorations and colours.

and the Vincennes (or Sèvres) factories were the leaders in their field and indeed established standards and fashions that all sought to copy. Their well-known factory marks –the crossed swords and the crossed "L" device– were widely copied by other makers as their significance was well known and accepted as a sign of quality.

The names of these pioneers are still widely respected today although naturally they have lost some of their one-time pre-eminence as the products of other later makers now appeal equally to discriminating buyers. Wedgwood, Minton or Royal Worcester in England, Haviland in France –you can compile your own short list of respected names–. One of the most recent to join this list will, of course, be Lladró of Spain.

I have in this short résumé of European porcelains mentioned the leading German and French firms. There were also other respected centres in other countries, some of which enjoyed a lasting reputation. One that remains today —at least in its basic name— is the Italian porcelain factory at Capodimonte which was founded in 1743.

Another important Italian factory was located at Doccia near Florence. This dates from about 1737 and is associated with Marquis Carlo Ginori. The Doccia porcelain is typically of a greyish tone with a very glossy glaze.

There were also porcelain factories at Venice. The first flourished in the mid-1720s. Another was established in about 1757. The largest and best known at Venice was that managed by Germiniano Cozzi which finally closed in 1812. These Cozzi period Italian porcelains are of a rather grey tone with a glassy covering glaze. The mark employed was an anchor device painted in red enamel which has often been mistaken for the more commercially desirable Chelsea anchor mark even though the English version is far smaller and more neatly rendered than its Italian counter-part.

Until recent times little porcelain has been produced in Spain or in Portugal although both countries had thriving earthenware factories. The Spanish Buen Retiro soft-paste porcelains (c. 1760-1804), including figures, can be quite beautiful but the mix was changed to produce a hard-paste porcelain from 1804 to the closure in 1808. It should be noted that the former Buen Retiro moulds were re-used at La Moncloa near Madrid during the period 1817-1850. There was also a Spanish hard-paste factory at Alcora in the latter part of the eighteenth century. The original Italian Capodimonte porcelain works were transferred to Madrid in 1769 after Charles III had become King of Spain.

In Portugal some porcelains were made at the Royal Military Arsenal at Lisbon from about 1773; and in the nineteenth century the Vista Alegre works near Oporto made hard-paste porcelains from 1824. In general the Spanish and Portuguese had always favoured the Chinese true porcelains and both countries imported large quantities of Chinese export-market wares. In recent years, the Vista Alegre company has made a feature of very good copies of eighteenth century Chinese export market porcelains.

Considering the relatively small size of England it is remarkable how many porcelain factories it supported; all without the benefit of State or other wealthy backers. It is also remarkable how many inventions or innovations of great ceramic importance were English and the extent to which its wares

—earthenwares as well as porcelains— were exported throughout the world. By the nineteenth century, the English (if not the British) potters had replaced the Chinese as potters to the world!

This story, however, had very humble beginnings and sadly we do not know when it started. We have no firm fixed date, not even the year, when porcelain was first produced in England. The now generally accepted year is 1745, that is long after the great Continental factories had been established.

The first two English factories, those of Bow and Chelsea, were both situated in or near the capital. Bow to the East of the City of London, Chelsea to the West. Bow in particular sought to copy the popular Chinese imports which were unloaded from vessels berthed in the river Thames only a short distance from the new factory. The management went so far as to model their works on the English "Factory" or depot on the Canton waterfront. They also called their manufactory "New Canton". An early account of the factory, published in the 1748 edition of Daniel Defoe's *Tour of Great Britain,* reads:

> "...the first village we come to is Bow, where a large Manufactory of Porcelain is lately set up. They have already made large quantities of teacups, saucers, etc., which by some skilful persons are said to be little inferior to those which are brought from China...".

Most of the output was devoted to useful tablewares, in particular tea services. Many of the products were decorated in underglaze-blue as were the less expensive Chinese patterns. Good enamelled copies of some Chinese originals were also produced and were presumably still deemed saleable some fifty or more years after they were first introduced to Europe. Apart from tablewares the Bow factory also made attractive figures, animal models and groups. The Bow mix is of the soft-paste variety and includes calcined animal bones. The works closed in 1776.

The Chelsea factory was, we believe, established in or slightly before 1745. Certainly good, seemingly post-experimental, examples exist with the incised date 1745. Again, an early notice mentions the new English wares in connection with the popular Oriental imports:

> "We hear that the China made at Chelsea is arrived to such Perfection, as to equal if not surpass the finest old Japan...".
> (*Daily Advertiser*, March 5th 1745)

The Chelsea porcelains were aimed at a rather higher market than the Bow wares. Most attractive figures and elaborate groups were produced in addition to well potted and attractively painted tablewares. Very little blue and white was, however, made at Chelsea, in contrast to the policy adopted at Bow and at most other English factories. Some early figures and groups of the approximate period 1745-50 were left in the white undecorated state perhaps in emulation of the Chinese *Blanc de Chine* imports. The Chelsea body, although it was amended over the years, was always of the soft-paste type. The standard factory mark comprised an anchor device, painted in gold during the later years. The Chelsea porcelains have for long been famous and collectable and very many later copies have been made, mostly on the Continent in a hard-paste porcelain. The reader is referred to the several specialist books on Chelsea porcelain or to recent general reference books such as Geoffrey Godden's *Eighteenth Century English Porcelain* (Granada Publishing, London, 1985). The Chelsea factory was taken over by William Duesbury of the Derby factory in 1769.

A small but important English porcelain factory was established in the City and port of Bristol in 1749. The proprietors were Benjamin Lund and William Miller. Lund was one of the earliest porcelain manufacturers (if not the first) to include Cornish soaprock (hydrated magnesium silicate) in their mix. This addition seemingly eased the manufacturing process and resulted in a pleasing soft-paste type of porcelain, usually having a slightly greenish translucency when held to the light. The useful wares produced at the so-called Lund's Bristol Works

Outstanding among English contributions to the art of porcelain are the creations by Wedgwood, which the author himself christened marbled clay.

comprise articles decorated in underglaze-blue with mock Chinese landscape designs. One somewhat primitive model of a Chinese *blanc de chine* standing figure was made. These rarities bear the moulded mark "Bristol 1750" on the back. The factory closed in 1751 when the secret of their process was sold to a group of merchants, etc. in Worcester.

In the Staffordshire Potteries at least two early attempts were made to produce porcelain. The first, of the approximate period 1746-1754, was at Newcastle-under-Lyme and here, on the site of what was later the Pomona Inn, a type of hybrid porcelain was made. Our key pieces, however, are spoiled *wasters* found there and no complete documentary examples have as yet been identified. The second attempt at porcelain making was rather more successful, being conducted by an experienced potter William Littler. His Longton Hall porcelain works produced between 1750 and 1760 a wide range of soft-paste porcelains including figures and groups and Meissen-style vegetable or fruit tureens or covered boxes for use on a table. The Longton Hall porcelains are rather thickly potted and bear no comparison with the Continental or the Chelsea products. The factory's output must have been large for the remaining stock when sold at auction in Salisbury in Southern England in 1760 comprised "upwards of ninety thousand pieces". As with most collectable English factories specialist reference books exist to guide the interested collector or student. In this case, one refers to Dr Bernard Watney's book *Longton Hall Porcelain* (Faber & Faber, London, 1957).

One of the most important English porcelain factories was that established in the City of Derby in or about 1750. The main partner, and later owner, was William Duesbury. Here the emphasis was not so much on copying Chinese or Japanese porcelains as on emulating Continental, mainly Dresden, porcelains, particularly their figures and groups. Indeed, the factory was termed the "Second Dresden"! Charming as the early Derby porcelains are, this was a somewhat optimistic claim and again the porcelain was of the soft-paste type not the hard-paste Continental mix.

The Derby porcelains were extremely diverse and of a uniformly high quality. The soft body and glaze is particularly pleasing both to the eye and to the touch. Some examples of the post-1870 period are very well painted with named views (sometimes of Continental scenes) whilst other pieces such as dessert services were attractively painted with botanical specimens. The unglazed white Derby porcelain figures and groups were particularly well modelled and potted. They are the English equivalent of the Sèvres white *bisquit* models. It is interesting to observe from the original price lists that the undecorated specimens were more costly than the glazed and painted examples of the same model. The explanation for this is that the extant white ones were those few examples that survived the firing process in an unblemished state. The slightly stained or cracked pieces could have their defects decently concealed by the added colouring.

The Derby factory was a large and prosperous one. The management in 1769 took over the famous Chelsea factory in London and they employed the leading modellers, artists and gilders. The factory was continued by William Duesbury's son and then by other owners and managers until 1848. Subsequently a small group of former Derby workpeople opened their own small factory in King Street and in 1876 a completely new porcelain factory was established in

Derby. After 1890 this became known as the "Royal Crown Derby Porcelain Company" and this continues to the present day.

The porcelain industry in the city of Worcester on the banks of the River Severn was established in 1751 when Dr John Wall and a group of local businessmen made what we would now term a take-over bid for Benjamin Lund's works at Bristol. Lund, probably with several of his workers, came up-river to found the new Worcester porcelain factory. This was blessed with success, all the experimental work having been undertaken and the process perfected previously at Bristol.

The Worcester porcelain was an extremely workable one with a good compact body and clear clean glaze. It is both durable and pleasant and lends itself to the various decorating processes. Like the Bristol mix it contains Cornish soap rock and has a greenish translucency when held to the light.

Much of the early Worcester porcelain shows a decided Oriental flavour, both the neatly painted underglaze-blue designs and the tasteful overglaze enamelled patterns. The shapes, however, are mostly English rather than Oriental and the relief-moulded forms, for teawares, sauce-boats, etc. owe much to the contemporary silver shapes.

The technique of printing on ceramics is claimed as an English invention and certainly the Worcester essays in this medium show great accomplishment and charm. Most of the more attractive and skilled engravings for over-glaze decoration were the work of Robert Hancock and some of his designs bear his signature or initials. Overglaze printing at Worcester had reached a very high standard by 1757.

Printing in blue under the glaze presents more problems than overglaze printing and the process was probably not introduced until the early 1760s. It was not as artistically successful as the overglaze method but it did enable long runs of standard patterns to be produced at a relatively low cost and so find a ready sale. Printed designs should not be despised, much skilled hard work goes into the engraving of the copper-plates and great care has to be exercised in transferring the impression. A good well-engraved print is surely superior to a poor hand-painted design.

The vast majority of the eighteenth century Worcester porcelains comprise neat tablewares. Very few figures were made and there are probably no more than five or six models. Later in the century a second important porcelain factory was established in Worcester. This is known as Chamberlains-Worcester. It was established in 1785 and effectively took over the larger main Worcester company in 1840. A third factory was established by Thomas Grainger early in the nineteenth century and later several other smaller works were set up.

The city and port of Liverpool was an important ceramic centre in England. Tin-glazed and other earthenwares were produced before the porcelains which date from the mid-1750s onwards. Several different small factories catered here for both the home and the export markets. Each concentrated on the production of low or medium priced useful wares. Much of the Liverpool porcelain is decorated in underglaze-blue and many mock-Chinese designs are to be found on the unmarked products of these factories. Liverpool was also a centre of the ceramic printing industry and several types of pottery and porcelain were sent there to be printed by Messrs Sadler & Green.

The small East coast town of Lowestoft also boasted a small factory where soft-paste porcelains, containing in the mix calcined bones, were made within the period 1757-1799. A large part of these Lowestoft porcelains was painted in underglaze-blue usually, but not exclusively, with Oriental-styled formal landscape or floral designs. The enamelled porcelains also tended to emulate the ever popular Chinese export market porcelains. This small factory, whose management was also engaged in the local herring curing trade, gained fame and notoriety in the nineteenth century when some early authorities attributed to this soft-paste factory the mass of imported Chinese true porcelains. Even today the name "Lowestoft" or "Chinese Lowestoft" is incorrectly used when describing a certain type of Chinese porcelain.

It must be borne in mind that up to about 1770, even with all the English porcelain factories in full production, there was probably more Chinese porcelain in use in the British Isles than there were our own productions. The balance was later to swing dramatically in the other direction particularly when, in the early 1790s, the English East India Company ceased its bulk imports of Chinese porcelain, leaving this trade to the private adventures of the ships' captains, supracargoes and crews.

There exists a rare class of mid-eighteenth century Chinese porcelain which was painted and even printed in England. In the main this embellishment was carried out by talented independent decorators, the best known of whom was James Giles of London. The decoration of Oriental porcelain was also carried out on the Continent, particularly in Holland.

I have hitherto confined my account to English porcelain manufacturers, but there was also a china works in Scotland situated at West Pans, near Edinburgh, between about 1764 and 1777. This was carried on by William Littler who had earlier managed the Longton Hall factory in Staffordshire.

In my chronological survey of English porcelain manufacturers, we now come in the late 1760s to a landmark. This was the discovery in Cornwall of the two basic raw materials needed to produce true hard-paste porcelain. This breakthrough is credited to William Cookworthy, an apothecary in Plymouth. After initial experiments he established his Plymouth porcelain factory in 1768. Great difficulties were experienced in successfully firing unblemished white porcelain and the works closed after only two years when the venture was transferred to Bristol. Here the firing difficulties seem to have been largely overcome and, in 1774, William Cookworthy sold out to his partner Richard Champion who continued the Bristol factory until 1780 or 1781. William Cookworthy was one of the very few English potters to have enjoyed some protection from the Government. He has been granted a Patent which in effect gave him exclusive rights to use the combination of china clay and china stone to produce porcelain. Richard Champion was later to sell these rights to a group of potters in Staffordshire, leading to the formation of the important New Hall Company at Shelton in the Staffordshire Potteries.

Because of the protection given by these Patent rights or perhaps on account of the difficulty of firing the hard-paste porcelain at the requisite high temperature, very few English manufacturers sought to produce these high-fired porcelains. Even after the discovery of hard-paste raw materials in Cornwall,

Lladró porcelain is the heir of those porcelains that, a millennium ago, were created in the Orient, although European methods have been incorporated into that ancient art.

most English manufacturers continued to produce the traditional soft-paste English china, sometimes with added calcined bones and at other times with the addition of soaprock.

Although from the middle of the eighteenth century onwards some English porcelain makers had added to their soft-paste mixes a proportion of burnt (calcined) bones, it was not until about 1800 that the English "Bone China" as we know it today, was first introduced by Josiah Spode in the Staffordshire Potteries. This improved mix comprised the China Stone and China Clay (of true porcelain) with up to fifty percent of calcined bones. The resulting body is both strong and beautiful. From the potter's point of view it was workable and dependable, being relatively easy to produce, to shape and to fire successfully. It also lent itself well to the various decorating processes.

In England the "bone china" porcelains had superseded all others by about 1816 and even today it is practically the standard only type of porcelain made in the British Isles for use on the table or for decorative purposes.

In about 1820 a slight amendment was introduced by some English firms, notably at the Coalport factory in Shropshire and by the Spode factory in Staffordshire. The newly introduced material was Felspar. This gave a softer effect, the porcelain and the glaze having a pleasing warm feeling and the added surface colours partly sunk into the glaze giving a mellow effect.

In the early 1840's a new ceramic body was introduced in the Staffordshire Potteries, primarily for the production of miniature copies of famous marble statuary. This body containing China clay

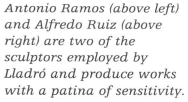

Antonio Ramos (above left) and Alfredo Ruiz (above right) are two of the sculptors employed by Lladró and produce works with a patina of sensitivity.

Salvador Furió (right) has the rare ability to conceive figures with a great sense of monumentality, despite their small dimensions.

Previous page, José Puche (above) and Vicente Martínez (bottom). The former creates with an intellectual style in an

ornamental tradition, while the work of the latter, with his talent for minute detail, is uncomplicated and tender.

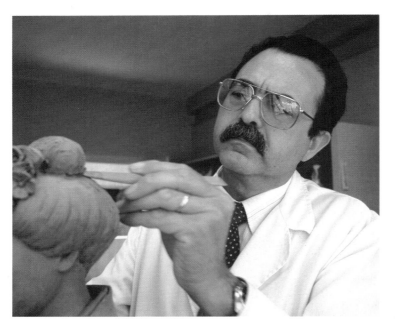

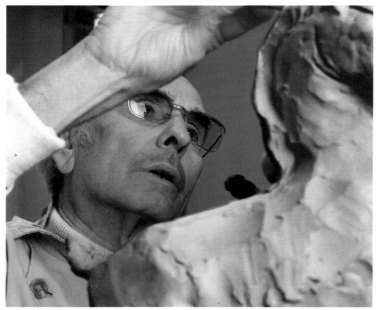

Francisco Catalá (above) endows his feminine figures with Mediterranean classicism.

Fulgencio García (bottom) produces works with a great refinement.

Julio Fernández (above) produces artistic creations of great strength and consistency. Juan Huerta

(bottom) works with such sureness that his works seem to flow effortlessly out from his hands.

and felspar, was at first called "Statuary Porcelain" but later all firms adopted the name "Parian", because of its marble-like appearance.

The parian figures and groups soon proved to be extremely popular even although they were white not coloured. Some models were reduced copies of antiques and of famous marble statues etc. Other often quite charming examples were especially modelled by leading sculptors and modellers of the Victorian period. Once the original model had been produced, a series of moulds would be made for the different parts: the head, body, hands etc. and the units made separately by the slipcasting method. These various pieces were then carefully luted together and the joints very carefully smoothed, so producing a graceful replica of the original. The basic methods of manufacture are very similar to those employed to produce the modern Lladró figures and groups —wellproven, traditional methods that have been much the same for the hundreds of years past—. As with these

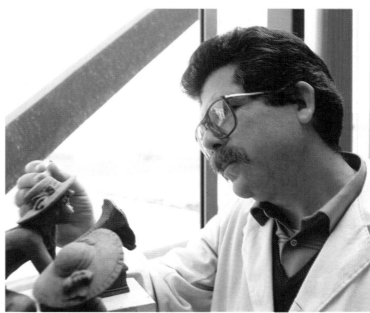

Salvador Debón (above) is gifted with a rare acuteness which he is unique in being able to apply to his small sculptures. Regino Torrijos (below) is a master of the difficult art of detail.

The application of colour is a task of such delicacy that it can be entrusted only to highly experienced, expert hands, such as those of Lladró craftsmen, who have managed to master the different processes with love and enthusiasm. The success of these pieces is due largely to the quality of their colour.

modern figures the leading manufacturers of parian and bone-china figures marked their productions with their names —as a guarantee of quality—. Some modern Lladró essays reflect the charm of the Victorian parian figures.

I have explained that the very porcelain of which the present-day Lladró figures are made, is no novel new material —it is related to the ancient Chinese true porcelains, although the Spanish body will be more refined due to modern techniques—. The basic methods of production are little different from those employed in China or at Meissen in Germany or at Chelsea in London or indeed at any other now internationally known porcelain factory which specializes in figure production: Doulton, Royal Worcester or Copenhagen.

How then do the Lladró porcelain statuettes differ from all the others, from the antique and more recent models made by many other firms. You will shortly be reading the history of this so individual concern —one of the very few that have ever concentrated so successfully on ornamental figures and groups—. For almost without exception other now famous factories established themselves in the production of useful objects: tea services, dinner services etc. before turning to make purely decorative articles, not so the Lladró brothers.

You will be able to see from the illustrations the charm of the creations, the grace of the models, the diversity of the subjects and the very high quality control that has so obviously been applied to all stages of the production of each specimen. The Lladró underglaze colours add a delicacy that is lacking in the traditional porcelain figures where the enamels are added over the glaze resulting in a rather harsh effect.

What this book cannot achieve, although it can guide you towards it, is the joy and sense of pleasure that you will obtain by owning a Lladró model or by starting a small personal collection.

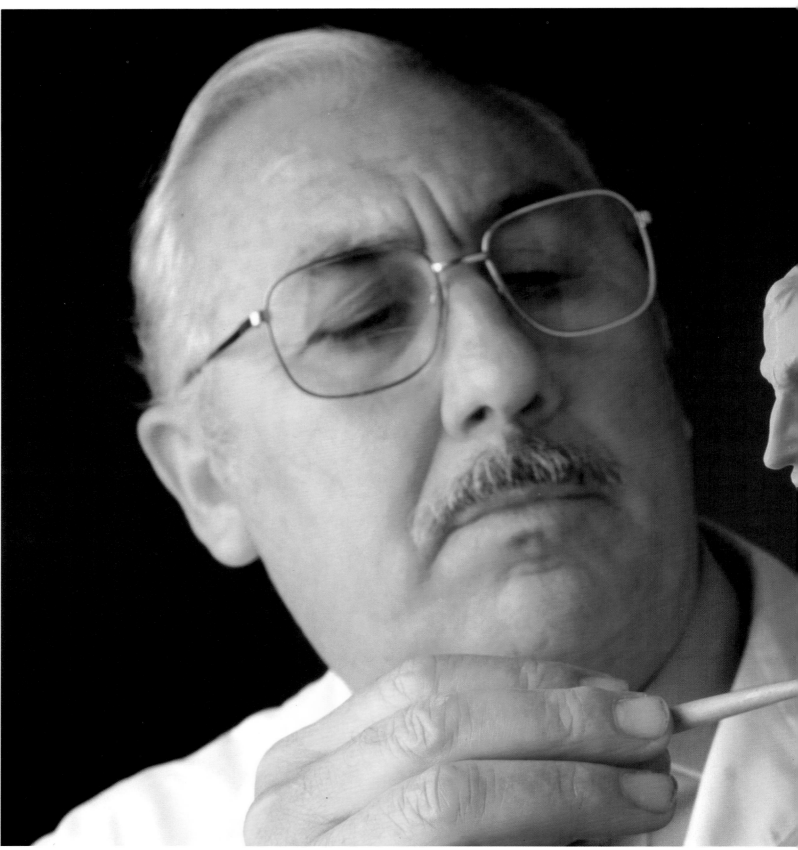

How a work of art is created

It is said that works of art contain something of a mystery, above all those that, at least in appearance, seem simple to us. It is often difficult to understand that a small object can contain exquisite beauty and a rare perfection. Often, however, on making these considerations, it is not a question of beauty in itself, since this is a subject we shall not touch here, but rather of how it has been reached, how it has been achieved, what fountains of inspiration have been drunk from, and what luminous paths have been followed so that we may now contemplate it. Some prefer to remain in ignorance of this genesis of beauty for fear of becoming disillusioned, and there are those who are not interested in it since they feel it is unnecessary: they are satisfied with beauty as the result of the creation of a work or with knowing that it is, quite simply, that marvellous property which is only possessed by certain objects.

However, neither attitude should be accepted as definitive principles or as something absolutely certain, since disillusionment need not be the end result of knowledge, and there is no reason why

*As can be appreciated
on these pages, the
task of sticking on
and the finishing
touches to the
different pieces that
together will form one of
the most exquisite Lladró
pieces require intense
concentration and can
only be entrusted to
expert hands.*

The modelling of different fragments and the obtention of the corresponding hollows both have to be carried out with painstaking care if the final result is to be perfect.

knowing how a work of art is created should reduce by one iota its power to seduce.

For this reason the Lladró brothers, undisputed creators of a form of beauty always clad in sobriety and good taste, have not hesitated in revealing the process by means of which their porcelains, genuine works of art, are produced. Their realisation is not swallowed up in the fog of mystery; on the contrary it states quite clearly the extent to which the creative capacity of these men can go. Furthermore, they are now receiving a new contribution which will undoubtedly prove to be highly fecund: the entry into the lists of the second generation of Lladró, their children who, with the same principles and the same creative drives as their parents, but with the new thrust of youth, will contribute new support and possibly even more creative capacity.

The Lladró workshops are a cenacle of artists. Here ideas are hatched and the first lines of projects are drawn. It is the first seed... a seed with a deeply spiritual centre. It is the idea in the mind of the artist, which will first of all be sketched on paper and later, moulded into a figure by his hands.

This first phase of the process is always more or less the same, since it is the force of an idea that, transformed into the physical impulse of the artist himself, moulds the clay and imprints upon it those features and characteristics that had gradually been acquiring an inner life. This first sketch is minutely analysed in order to gauge all its characteristics, its successes and failures, in order to foster the former and eliminate the latter.

This is the moment when the dangerous, risky decision-making process comes into the fore: should one go on, rectify or reject totally?

It is the Lladró brothers themselves who, applying the criteria forged throughout their long training, encourage the contributions that each artist is able to offer, in order to enrich the models which emerge from their workshops without interrupting the unity of style which characterises their work as a whole. Thus, even when the work is collective, it's possible to speak accurately of the existence of the "author's stamp", the LLADRÓ stamp.

Returning to the recently modelled figure in clay, once it has been accepted a master model is produced and copied in plaster, and this will become the nucleus around which all the creation phases of the work will revolve. For this reason, the model must have all the details, even the most insignificant, of the final work, and it is on this model that the decision will be made on how the figure is to be cut up, for, indeed, the figure in question, which in this case is the well-loved Don Quixote, is divided up into several fragments from which the moulds will later be made. It is into these moulds that the porcelain paste is placed, having been prepared previously in the Chemistry Department of the company according to formulae which are the firm's greatest secret. The moulds are previously moistened and the paste, now inside, is allowed to dry slowly. This is a critical moment in the process since the quality of the final product will depend on how successful the drying process is. When the paste reaches the right consistency, the porcelain reproductions of the fragments are taken out of their respective moulds and are passed into the hands of craftsmen who, first of all, will reject the defective pieces and then painstakingly polish those that are considered perfect. Later, each of these elements which were separated from the figure under production will be fitted back together again with maximum precision. Thus, the head of the *hidalgo* from La Mancha will once again have to bow as before; his thin legs have to recover the effect of exhaustion given them originally by the artist, and the arm holding the sword must fall almost vertically to give the same impression of weariness and lassitude. This is another of the delicate, dangerous phases of the operation.

The pieces that have thus been fitted together to form the complete figure now pass into the hands of the painters. By virtue of their perfect knowledge of how colours behave, these men foresee the changes a particular colour will undergo during firing, and the shadows which will later be produced by the effects of light. Similarly, they know which colours best suit each figure. In the case of our knight-errant, for example, rosy colours on his face or gay colours on his clothes would be highly unsuitable. Our Knight of the Sorrowful Countenance must have a sallow complexion and sport dignified, though modest, clothes. Here, then, colour plays a very prominent role, and for this reason the intervention of the painters is of paramount importance for the final result. In general, the colouring on all porcelain pieces is always a decisive factor when it comes to evaluating the quality and beauty of each one; and it goes without saying that it is one of the most highly esteemed characteristics of Lladró

porcelains. The task of painting and varnishing these figures is a kind of artistic slap on the back received by the piece, and it is a task that can be carried out only by a specialist. These painters are the men who give those pigmentations and those pastel tones that seem to be exclusive characteristics of Lladró porcelain. Such colour is never vivid or even accentuated; it is rather a suggestion, like the beginnings of a blush or the gentle glow in the sky just before dawn.

The varnish is sprayed on in a coat that must neither be too thick nor too thin: once more precision and moderation become fundamental ingredients for these porcelain figures.

When each piece has its definitive colour, those that are to be shiny are separated from those that will have a matt finish. The latter, apparently simpler, perhaps for this very reason enhance the plasticity of form as the principal attribute of the work. The shiny pieces are more decorative.

The painted and varnished pieces still have to undergo the final test, what we might quite literally call the "baptism by fire": they have to be placed in the kiln and fired. And once again we are faced with a new phase in this chain of functions, each one complementing the other, and each one carried out in such a way as to ensure maximum perfection and to eliminate all possibility of error. Indeed, firing is yet another of the crucial moments in the manufacture of porcelain figures. It is a step which, if false, can prove to be fatal. A badly-regulated kiln can destroy in a matter of minutes the painstaking labour of months: the creation of the form by the sculptor, its modelling, cutting, drying of the

After having obtained the different fragments, they are then assembled with infinite care, since it is on this process that the degree of perfection of the final result depends.

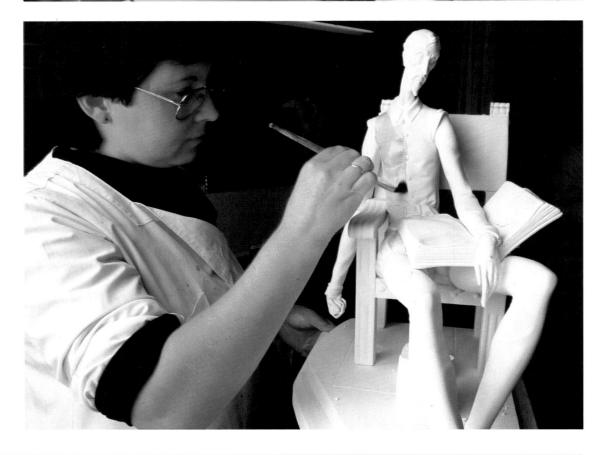

Once the figure has been assembled the painter highlights its most interesting and expressive details by means of the painstaking application of colour by hand. Gentle pastel shades are among the most esteemed of these colours on porcelain.

Next the figure is carefully varnished (above).
Once the piece has been finished and fired (right), it does
not have to wait long in the warehouse before being sent
to its destination anywhere in the world.

Before being sent to its new home, the delicate Lladró porcelain piece is properly packed in order to prevent its suffering any damage during the journey.

porcelain in the moulds, polishing, painting, varnishing, everything... Fortunately, however, this never happens. The true specialist knows the degree of temperature each piece can withstand and the kind of kiln in which it can be fired. Extreme heat reduces slightly the size of the pieces, but it is what finally gives them life. Fire at times creates rather than destroys.

And in this case it has created a truly remarkable piece, since the one we have taken here somewhat as our point of reference is none other than the great Spanish and universal figure of Don Quixote of La Mancha. What a challenge for the artist: to represent in porcelain the complex personality of the immortal knight-errant! For there can be no doubt that depending on the figure which the artist wishes to represent, to the aforementioned difficulties must now be added those connected with giving the true character and correct personality features to a famous personage, even if this personage is from fiction. There is a great difference between reproducing the figure of a bird or an animal, or even that of an anonymous man or woman, and expressing, for the future and by means of facial features, the inner world of a figure from the past and moreover of such psychological depth as our knight-errant.

The gentleman from La Mancha appears to us here at the beginning of his poetical insanity, when he spent night after sleepless night and each day was a new torment. His lanky figure is seated on an austere Castilian chair and his posture and the expression on his face are both evidence of the perfect conception and realisation of this work. On the knight's lap lies one of those novels of chivalry that filled his mind with fantasies. And no doubt he has reached a most interesting passage, since his demeanour reveals a certain moment of abstraction in what is otherwise a passionate reading. His left arm rests on the open volume, as if indicating the point where he left off, while his right arm brandishes, somewhat weakly, his hidalgo's sword, the sword that has not yet fought against giants and monsters but will not be long in doing so. He does not hold it now with the haughtiness with which he will do so later; one might say that here he is merely holding it just to feel it in his hand, while the point rests on the floor as the result of his deep introspection. His face expresses the same, or almost the same, as the crestfallen posture of the body. His is the face of someone who looks inwards rather than outwards, who looks without seeing. The gentleman has interrupted his reading to meditate on what he has read; now he does not see the book resting on his knees, he only sees inwardly what his reading has suggested.

Both the posture of the body and expression on the face have been fully achieved in this porcelain piece. And they have been achieved through each and every one of the different phases in the creation process, from the first clay model to the final heat of firing. The posture of the body was properly sketched in the first model and was modified in subsequent operations. And the painters took it upon themselves to ensure that this Don Quixote would have the pale complexion characteristic of a person who eats little and sleeps less and that his clothes would be the modest garb of a hidalgo of scant means.

And what has been done to reproduce in porcelain this great figure from Castilian literature is repeated in each and every Lladró porcelain piece, from the smallest, most insignificant animal to the representation of an august personage or the luxurious horse-drawn carriage of the nineteenth century. A work of art will always be a work of art whatever its size or subject matter.

Thus, with this constant desire for new levels of perfection, with this ethic applied to aesthetics, with this insistence on granting the same dedication to every piece and with this admirable tenacity with which they maintain all these principles in a living, fecund creation process, the Lladró brothers have managed to give their works that quality characteristic of great art that allows them to be recognised from among the work of others almost at first sight.

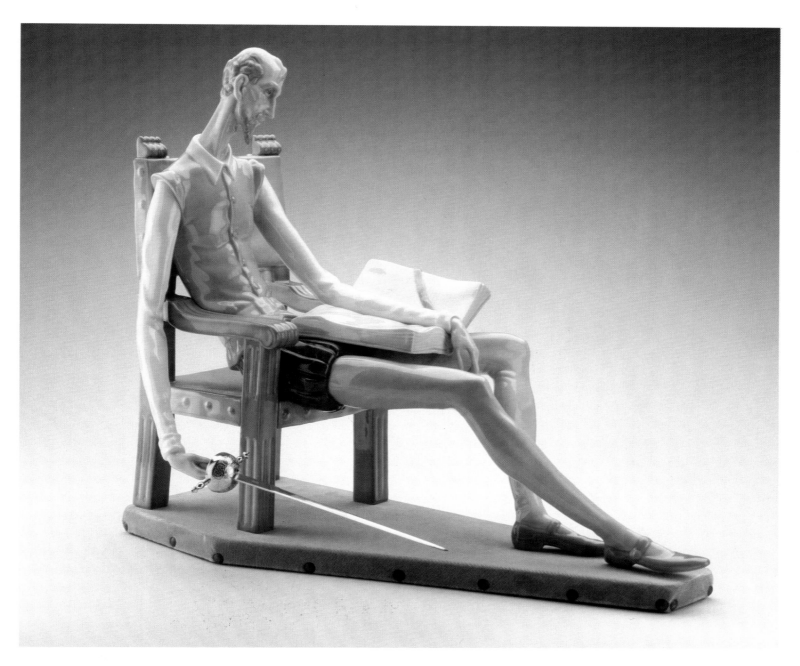

The figure of Don Quixote is finished and the colours well-matched. The stylised knight-errant, lost in the reverie induced by his obsessive reading, is about to embark upon his mission of "putting wrongs to right".

YEARS THAT ARE HISTORY

Almost forty years have passed since in 1951 the Lladró brothers began, modestly then and with genuine difficulties of all kinds, their activities as creators of porcelain. Depending on how they are considered or with what activity they are associated —without referring to history as a whole— these years are not many, but they *are* when seen in the context of the development of a human activity and allow one to speak of a genuine past of the same activity.

This time permits many initiatives, many trials and errors, many rectifications to be made, in addition to a long trajectory along which to exploit any success one may achieve, and which has certainly been achieved, totally and absolutely, in the case of Lladró porcelain. As has already been said, the first years were difficult; years of

experiment, of efforts to achieve a personal way of doing things, quality in the works and, above all, a distinctive style which would be the culmination of so much sleeplessness. Almost fifteen years were spent in the search for a personal, distinctive form of expression and for a good product that would be different from others and enjoy a wide market. But they were fifteen fertile years, wonderfully fertile years, since they were the crucible in which ideas, projects, tests and trials and comparisons were forged in the heat of three truly creative spirits, liberally mixed with large doses of a recently achieved reality. A fusion in which finally a style was forged and a work was structured: the unmistakable Lladró style and a great enterprise on an international scale.

The works produced then, during those first

The grace of this young lady centres on her lively face and her startled posture.

years which now seem historical to us and which, undoubtedly, in terms of the course followed by Lladró porcelain, really are years that belong to the firm's history, are works that despite their not yet thoroughly defined style already had their own character, their own profile, which already "shout out" what they were shortly to become.

Just as a painter applies a brush-stroke to his canvas, a single brush-stroke that nevertheless completely defines his style and reveals the identity of his hand; or as a couturier accentuates a pleat or gives a special touch to the way a dress is made converting the garment into a model; so the Lladró brothers managed to create, from the very beginning, those pieces which by some unknown miracle already had that particular imprint, that characteristic style, that combination of flexibility, langour and elegance which later, strengthened with the passing of years, was to acquire all the value of a definitive personality.

The pieces that appear on these pages belong to this first period, and contemplation of them can

A young sportswoman has sat down to rest after her exertions. While resting she takes a certain interest in her surroundings and now looks attently around, though her posture cannot disguise a certain indifference.

only corroborate what has already been said about then above. It may even be that someone unversed in the subject will be unable to distinguish these first works from those produced recently.

The first of this series of illustrations shows the figure of a young girl, about to become a woman, whose girlish tresses seem already to be a memory of her infancy that stubbornly remains, perhaps with a certain nostalgia, upon a pair of adult shoulders. The girl is sitting on the ground and the posture of her body, in repose with legs outstretched, as well as the somewhat petulant toss of the head, are features characteristic of Lladró porcelain.

The human figure is ever-present on these pages, and that of the woman occupies a crucial position. Ladies from periods in the past, dressed in the fashion of the time reproduced with exquisite precision and fidelity, appear repeatedly. A young woman in the rich costume of the XVIIIth century is seated on a country bench and her full

The flautist is a piece where different traditions meet. On the one hand there is a clear reminiscence of Graeco-Roman statues, while on the other a certain negligent air characteristic of the works of Watteau.

This ballerina is a miracle of artistic creation. Besides the marvel of her lace costume and the daring balance on only one foot, the sensation of movement is very intense, since the position of her arms reveals that she is about to do a pirouette, or has just completed one. Whatever the case, the feeling of movement has been perfectly captured.

The four figures on the opposite page, though their positions and costumes are quite different, are all examples of admirable solutions to a particular problem: the incorporation of lace into porcelain.

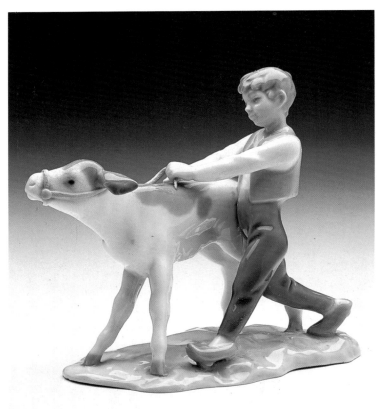

In these pieces we see three different representations of children. Above, in the group of the young shepherd and the lamb the combination of child and animal is very well modelled.

Above, the hesitant first steps have been captured in white porcelain.

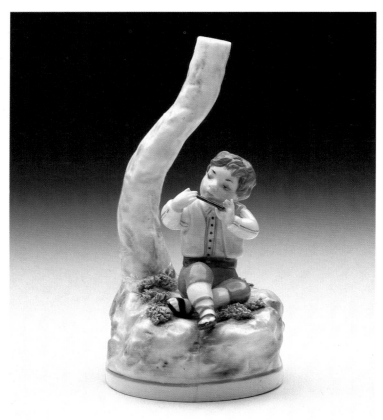

On the left, the little shepherd-boy plays his instrument as he rests after a hard day's work.

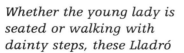

Whether the young lady is seated or walking with dainty steps, these Lladró *porcelain figures are a hymn to eternal femininity.*

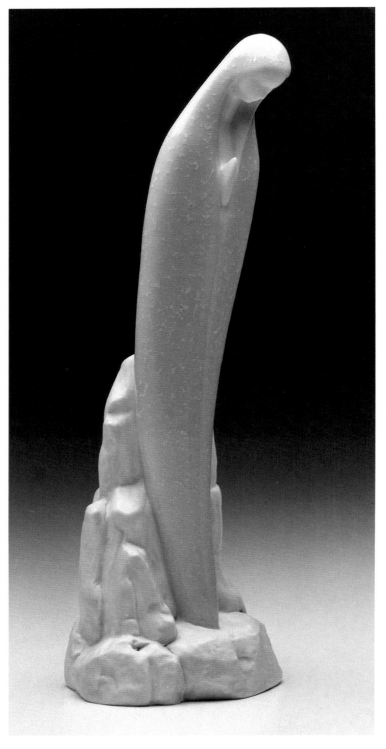

dress flows to the ground in wide, beautiful folds, to which the artist has managed to give a most realistic appearance. Other ladies, also from the seventeen-hundreds, remind us of those of the court of Marie Antoinette with their high coiffures, generously low necks and skirts widened at the sides with the characteristic *paniers* of the period. Together with that of another lady dressed in the fashion of 1830, when Romanticism had spread over the whole of Europe, these feminine figures display a series of details which in order to be reproduced in porcelain required on the part of their creators extremely difficult, painstaking, even exhausting, work. But such figures, partly as a result of the very difficulty of their manufacture and partly as a result of their subject-matter, which evokes a courtly, refined world, are highly suitable pieces for decoration of the home and take their rightful places among all those objects that people like to have around them.

The same can be said of the figures of ballerinas, a very popular subject with the public

This figure of the Virgin preparing to pray in an attitude of intense absorption and modesty is an example of the stylization of figures in religious subjects.

which from the very beginning has enjoyed special attention from the Lladró brothers. It is a kind of porcelain that may perhaps seem to belong exclusively to a young girl's bedroom; nevertheless it can form an equally suitable part of the decoration of any sitting room where the family gather. These ballerinas, by virtue of their art, lend themselves admirably to the reproduction of postures in porcelain which are a genuine challenge to the artist who has to create them. Such grace in gesture and movement, so characteristic of dancers, constitutes a veritable tour de force of artistic skill. The artist had to fix the position, the gesture, but could only suggest the idea of movement in porcelain, something he has fully achieved not only in the figures actually dancing but also in the one sitting down who gives the impression that she has only just stopped or, rather, that she has not fully stopped and that she is looking for a comfortable position for her legs while moving her hands towards her lap in order to rest them there.

The costume of the ballerina executing a

The slenderness of the giraffe's neck contributes towards creating a sensation of elevation of the palm trunk.

complex pirouette on the tip of her toes opens out like the petals of a flower revealing a series of drawn work that is a genuine miracle of craftsmanship, a miraculous display of skill very characteristic of the first period of the Lladró company.

It was in the realisation of ballerina figures that the tendency to elongate the human form was developed as a characteristic with which to stylize figures —even religious ones— giving them a new dimension that places them at a far remove from vulgarity and conferring upon them an elegant nobility. The dancer who is tying up the lace of her shoe, her foot resting on a stool, is irrefutable evidence of this: that outstretched leg and those arms reaching down could be those of a goddess of pagan antiquity.

Generally speaking the woman, and quite often the woman from past periods, is a subject which reappears with a certain frequency by virtue of the thousands of variations it offers. Women standing and sitting; women carrying out some task or other; women in pensive mood; women sporting regional costumes; each and every one of them in graceful postures, their costumes faithfully reproduced and their expressions highly realistic. The folds or fall of a skirt, hair dishevelled in the wind, the modesty of a village woman who covers her head and part of her face with her shawl or the ingenuous cheekiness of a young face beneath the brim of a small hat all display the technique and artistic inspiration of the first works offered by Lladró.

Within the field of the human figure, Lladró, in its rise to fame, never overlooked the figure of the child. By virtue of its very nature, the figure of the child cannot be represented in the same ostentious way as that of, say, eighteenth-century ladies. Therefore the Lladró brothers opted to represent it highlighting those characteristics most typical of childhood: innocence and spontaneous, ingenuous charm. The child sometimes appears alone, sometimes in the company of animals, sometimes in groups, and sometimes as a chubby angel with puffed out cheeks so reminiscent of the *putti* or cupids from the distant times of rococó. Be this as it may, however, the aforementioned characteristics dominate, which are the very essence of the infant soul. And, just like the ballerinas or the eighteenth-century ladies, these children have their rightful place in any room in any home.

The animals that appear with the children are, as one might expect, small animals: a puppy, a cat, a bird, a duckling; occasionally the children appear with a bear cub, an animal that perhaps reminds them of their favourite toy, and, exceptionally, with a calf. These animals, however, are always just like the children: at the beginning of their life and lacking, as yet, strength and aggressivity. And although a calf, even if it is newly born, is much bigger than a child, its feebleness and gentleness allow the child, like the one in the illustration, to hold it and keep it by his side, albeit by means of quite an effort.

Animals as the main protagonists of Lladró porcelain pieces began to figure in catalogues from the very beginning of the firm's activities. There can be no doubt that certain animals have a magnificent appearance so that the temptation to

The singing angels treat the Boy Jesus to an improvised concert, who is worshipped and watched over by one of them. At one end one of the angels has fallen asleep beside the ruins of the doorway, like a mischievous child.

These three figures are joined together in an explosion of colour. Thus the parrot's plumage is an example of what can be done with vivid colours, while the girls show off their variegated regional costumes.

The baroque putti *have become one of the most interesting subjects for small-scale porcelain sculpture by virtue of the great range of possibilities they offer. These two, with their amusing postures, are a delight to the eye.*

The acolyte and the ballerina are two new creations of the art of representing children, *which are a delicious imitation of the postures of the little boys.*

*This masterpiece could be entitled "The Sportsman".
An extraordinarily athletic and vigorous boy has left the
bat and ball on the ground and, while resting, he has turned
to contemplate something that attracts his attention and
which causes him to smile slightly.*

Here we contemplate a masterpiece of small sculpture. The effect of the flight of these ducks in double file has been achieved by resting the bird above on the wing edge of the one below, a veritable miracle of balance.

The ballerina, who is giving the finishing touches to her shoes, forms a geometrical composition in which her body, her arms, her leg resting on the floor and an imaginary line joining both shoes, form an almost perfect square which the other leg crosses in diagonal. The straight lines of the floor and the top of the partition, which are perfectly horizontal, contribute to the dynamism of the piece.

reproduce them in porcelain, using the fine, traditional Lladró colours, is truly irresistible. Some, like the sitting cat with its long neck, are reproduced in a highly stylized way; nevertheless, those that figure most frequently are reproduced in a thoroughly realistic way, like these two splendid turtle doves, which, besides the remarkable balance of their composition, are so realistic in their plumage and in their suggested flight that they figure amongst the most successful pieces in this field. The same can be said of the impressive realism of the magnificent scene of the deer being pursued by the hounds.

The variety of the pieces belonging to the "years that are history", whether they are human or animal figures, alone or in groups, created with a purely decorative objective in mind, have their exceptional counterparts in a small number of pieces that, though they are no less decorative, also have a practical purpose. These are the original, exquisite table lamps whose stand is sometimes the figure of Harlequin, sometimes of Columbine, or on other occasions a showy, stylized animal. They are lamps which, even if they are never lit, are of a beauty that will always successfully carry out the decorative mission.

The group of porcelain pieces that figure on these pages constitutes, as has already been said, part of the legacy of the first years of the Lladró firm. As we contemplate them now, after so many years, we see clearly that these initial creations already offered with great artistic joy and generosity all the wealth of technique, of imagination and true art which has become crystallized in the splendid reality of today.

The positions of these two polar bears, just as we see them in zoological gardens, are a very positive contribution to animal themes in Lladró porcelain.

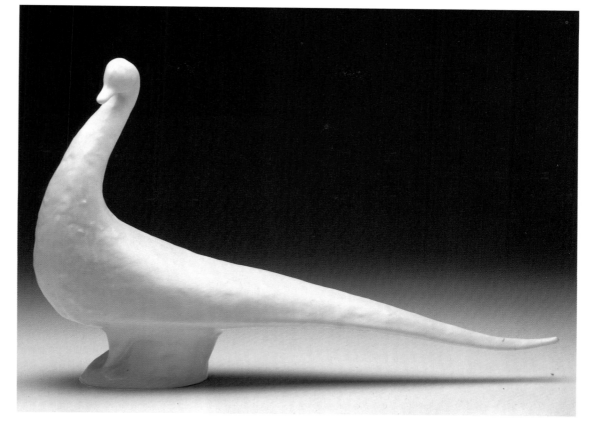

The common denominator of these pieces could be a kind of fantastic stylization, since the dimensions both of the bird's and the fish's tails have no connection with reality.

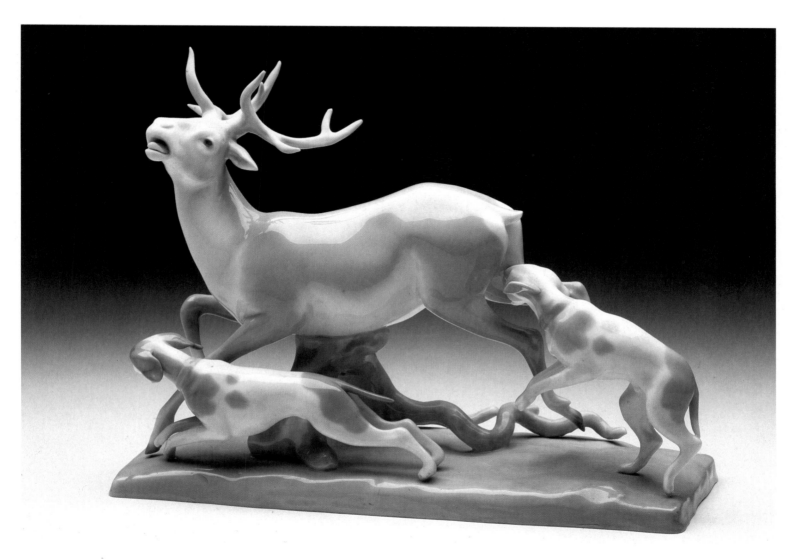

This Japanese pair are straight out of NO theatre, although their stylized figures have been achieved through contemplation by Western eyes. The subtle colour tones contribute to a certain air of unreality.

The deer hunt we see here is about to come to an end when the quarry, possibly wounded but above all tired, is prey to the dogs who will bring him to the ground. His head and horns raised towards the sky and his bellow, which we hear by intuition, clearly indicate that he knows he is going to die.

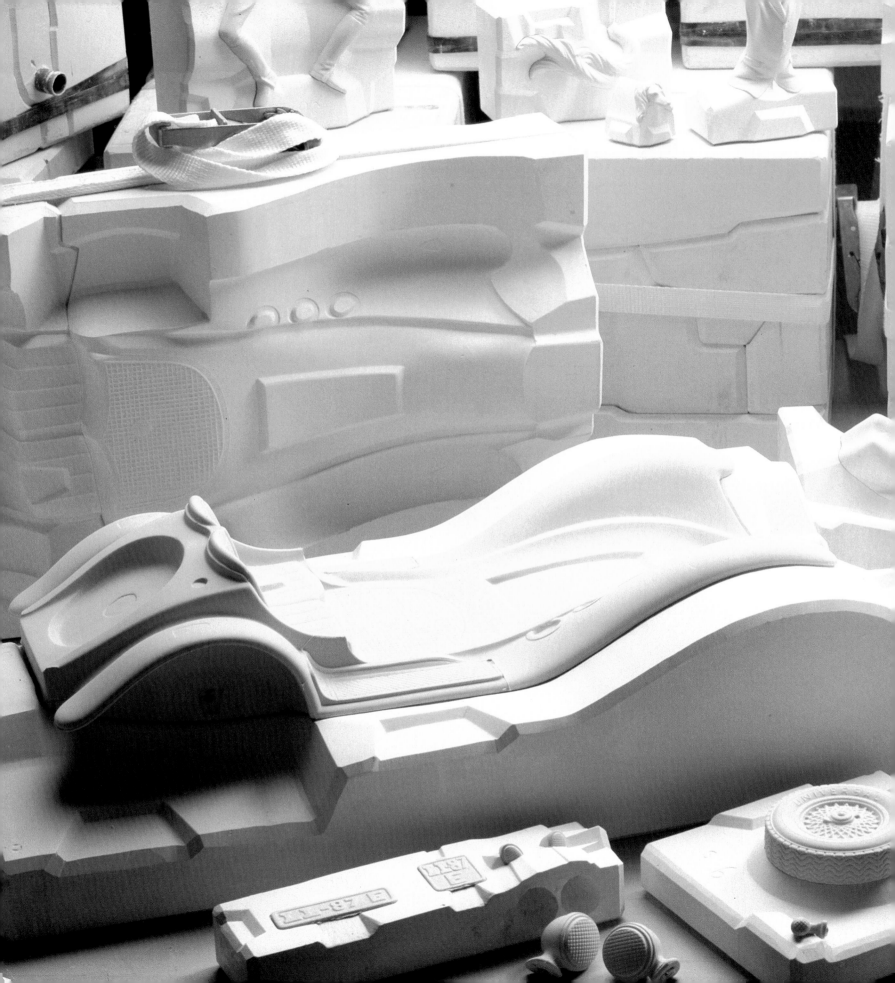

THE MOST RECENT HISTORY

On the contrary to happy peoples, who, it is said, have no history, successful enterprises *do* have one, since theirs is the history that their activities and progress have marked out on the road to success. Perfection in a work is never the result of a sudden radiance but of regular, constant, painstaking work. It is a whole trajectory and, for this reason, constitutes a small history. Without it the life of the company, companies themselves, would neither exist nor have the oportunity to exist.

The history of *Porcelanas Lladró* is brief but intense. Over the years the firm has structured very definite and distinct phases, each one highly individualised and, at each moment, new projects with precise, graded results. These phases were partly stages of preparation and of hard,

anonymous work, and partly periods of launching, of breaking into markets, of achievements and of consolidation.

This period of consolidation, to be followed by a new plenitude and the beginning of new directions, can be considered the most recent in the whole of the history of Lladró since it continued into the early eighties and was then followed by other periods which, though they are now enjoying a splendid zenith, are still in that upward moving spiral which will lead them to their final consagration.

The period in question appeared, being as I have said that of consolidation, with a series of very defined, concrete characteristics, the fruit of clear ideas wisely put into practice. One of these characteristics, which figures amongst the most

The warm humanity of circus performers
is reflected in this piece.

important, is the technical progress achieved during these years which have been equalled by no other firm devoted to the art of porcelain. And the astonishing level of perfection achieved in such advances was, as is always the case when the highest standards are aimed for, the fruit of long and laborious research undertaken by the Lladró brothers who for years worked completely alone, making test after test, experimenting with all kinds of possibilities, in order to reach that crucial nucleus which would then become the departure point and foundations for a whole artistic empire.

And upon this solid base constructed with so much effort other characteristics of the period began to manifest themselves which became and continue to be some of the most attractive facets of this porcelain. I am referring, on the one hand, to the astounding variety of subject matter that began to emerge then and, on the other, to the enormous variations of figure moulding. These qualities together and united became like a rich fertiliser that makes newly-sown earth so

An extraordinary group formed by the Three Kings of Orient, in which the faces of the wise men, the heads of the horses and the kings' cloaks constitute a veritable symphony of harmonious colours. This piece was given as a gift to Pope Paul VI.

The subject of animals was painstakingly treated here in this pair of gazelles who seem to have stepped out of space and time to remain eternally motionless in a kind of frozen dynamism. The effort of running and jumping become minimal beneath the elegance of wonderfully well modelled forms.

productive. Each new sculptural subject suggested almost immediately another, either deriving from it or in contrast to it; each new way of modelling gave rise to a variant of the same which, after a certain number of pieces had been produced, became a structure completely different from the one that preceded it. Thus, in this kind of geometrical progression of ideas and realisations that, like all progressions of this kind, grew and multiplied itself in an astonishing flight of creation, that great edifice of porcelain began to be built, that fantastic world composed totally of gentle profiles, harmonious colours and subtle, brittle shades...

And the artists of Lladró, in this agitated setting in which they worked, in which everything seemed to be cause and consequence at the same time, became subjected to increasingly more difficult demands; day by day they were obliged to make greater efforts in the technical and artistic fields in order to give satisfaction and solve the problems that their own fantasy and desire.for self excelling created. But these artists never ran away from such a challenge; on the contrary, they had

Motherhood in its widest sense is represented in this figure of a mother and son. Its extreme simplicity, in which there is no hint of superfluity, highlights the joyful serenity of the mother's face.

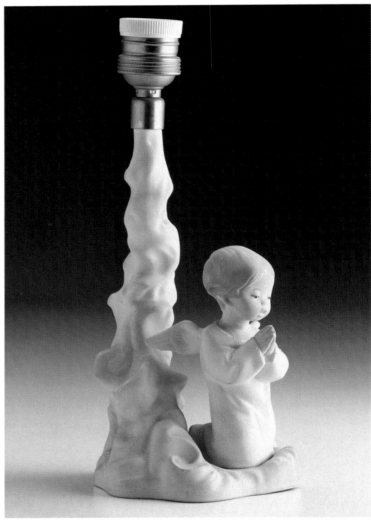

Figures of cherubim, one praying and the other two playing musical instruments, leaning against symbolic and functional trees, support for the bulb and the lampshade.

taken it up from the very beginning and accepted the responsibility, with pleasure, of making their role "even more difficult", as circus performers do. For it is precisely when faced with difficulties, faced with situations in which creative efforts must be doubled or new techniques be found, that the true standing of the artist and the true dimensions of his talent and cultural baggage can be revealed. And in this particular case the artists "created" the difficulty, went in search of it, measured it, solved it, defeated it and immediately, from its ashes, gave form to the next one.

Thus certain positions were reached which, from the technical point of view, are truly astounding. Some figures, for example, have the most unexpected support points; others, those that simulate action, give such an impression of movement, of life, that all that is needed is to be able to hear the wing beat, in the case of birds in full flight, or to hear the clatter of hooves on the ground if galloping horses are the subject. The search for new discoveries in all spheres was the overall keynote of this period; and it was thus because what governed all was precisely to surpass oneself in everything: in modelling, in the subject matter, in colour and in firing... Few are the occasions when an artist has to prove himself as such to the extent to which those of the Lladró workshops did at that time, when they were launched into the vertiginous double task of creating and producing.

It was at this time that the need arose, given the copious variety of subject matter, for a careful structuralisation and division of the figures into themes. Thus it was that the ten sections appeared

Decorative elements for these lampstands were sought among the characters of the Commedia dell'Arte, and the idyllic relationship between Harlequin and Columbine is represented in these stylised figures that harmonise perfectly with the verticality of the tree trunk separating them.

In contrast, the same characters have been treated differently in the case of these two lamps which together form a set (right). Not only have the lovers been separated, but also the verticality has been broken of the upright figures and tree by the horizontal position of Harlequin's violin and Columbine's skirt.

*These country folk, with their stylised, slender figures,
who seem to have been captured in a fleeting moment,
are a hymn to the industriousness of Valencian farmers.*

These water carriers, modelled with the stylisation and elongation of their figures, sway their bodies to give the piece an extraordinary sensation of elevation.

The two huntsmen who, accompanied by their dog, return from the hunt are an example of the most diverse activities becoming ideal subject matter for work in porcelain.

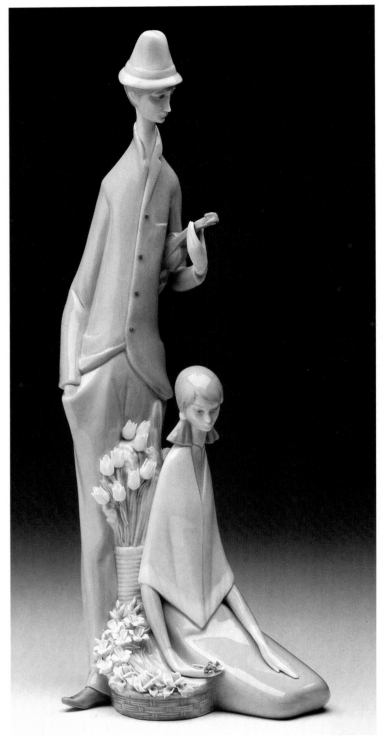

Though they belong to a bygone age, the components of this piece depicting nineteenth-century a couple playing with a puppy create an atmosphere of pleasant serene romanticism.

More suggestive, perhaps, by virtue of the dramatic connotations contained therein, is this incipient idyll between the street violinist and the young flower seller, who does not seem to predisposed to accept unequalled perfection the love she is being offered.

Both the nurse and the country woman represented on the right have been given slender, elongated figures in an attempt to transform them into the archetypes of these two professions.

In the representation of this couple of Flamenco dancers (bailaores) there is a remarkable balance between the male figure, projected like an arrow towards the sky, and the mass of the woman's skirt.

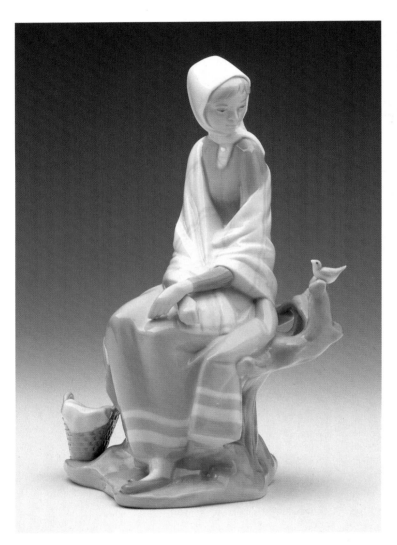

The two young peasant girls represented in these pieces (left) have one thing in common: their attention has been attracted by little animals. The former, tired perhaps after her long walk, converses with a small bird which has approached her without any hint of fear. The other watches closely as the little goose seems to attempt to jump out of the basket in order to join its mother.

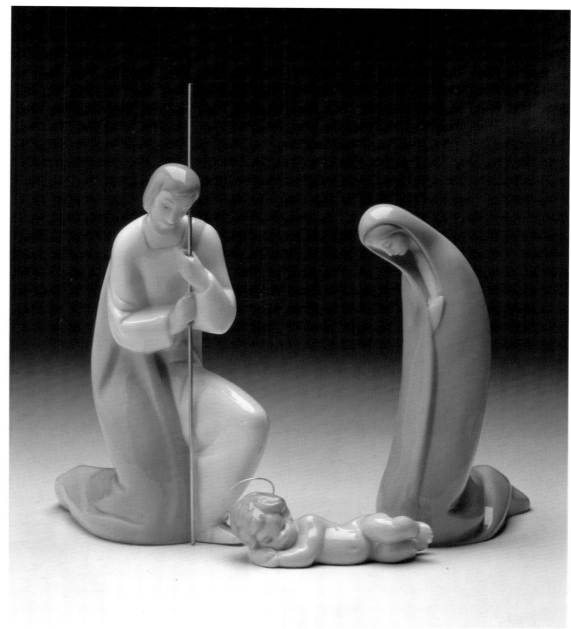

The subject of the Holy Family has been treated here from a double viewpoint: on the one hand, the traditional position of the Birth in Spanish Nativity scenes and, on the other, the modern conception of the figures of Joseph and above all Mary who here, except for the face, is reduced to a number of harmonious lines. This piece is one of the manifestations of the religious side of Lladró porcelain.

We have already seen that the world of clowns is by no means alien to Lladró porcelain. Of the pair reproduced here, the one above is in a typical posture, while the one at the side seems to be overcome with exhaustion.

The watchful postures of the swineherd and the shepherd (previous page) have been treated differently in this pair of figurines: the peasant woman looks after her piglets who stay close about her, while the shepherd gazes over the wide area where his herd is scattered.

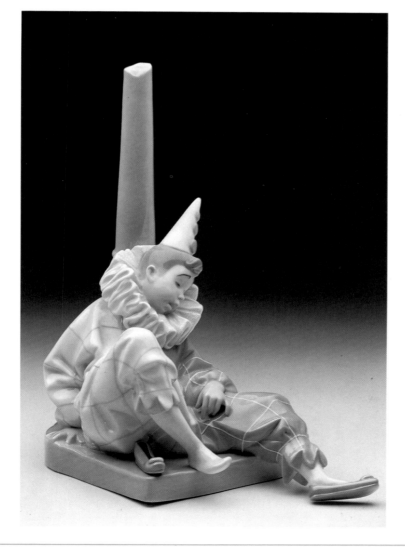

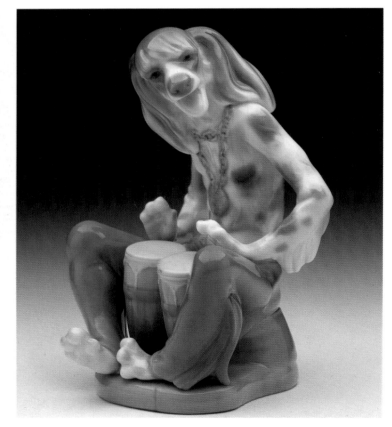

Creative fantasy, which allows combinations of the most disparate kinds, has brought into being these musical dogs which, contorting their bodies in a way which would be impossible in reality, play a variety of instruments.

A fine group in which Pierrot sings to a distracted Columbine in an attempt to win her love. She, in the meantime, pretends not to listen and seems to concentrate all her attention on the flower in her hands.

A noble Arabian horseman who, mounted on his short-legged horse, has exchanged his weapons for a bouquet of flowers.

which became, and still are, one of the most exquisite representations of the art of present-day porcelain. The first of these, *Customs and Everyday Life,* comprises a series of figures that, always remaining within the stylisation of Lladró porcelain, represent scenes from a given profession, activities of a particular social class, labours in the field, women's tasks, a shepherd, a sailor, a peasant woman; in other words, everyday scenes and characters interpreted through that vision that makes poetry out of reality, always avoiding any detail of trait that borders on sordidness, vulgarity or violence.

Dynamism, to which reference has already been made, is the keynote of the section in which groups of people or animals are represented achieving such a perfect sensation of movement that one realises immediately that only an exceptional mastery of the technique of modelling could produce such works. A group of footballers carrying out a difficult strategy, pairs of ballerinas dancing, hunting scenes and gazelles in full flight are irrefutable proof of this.

Animals have a section all to themselves *Animals in Porcelain,* and it is here that the capacity for observation and the faculty for reproducing what is observed reach heights of pure delight. Dogs and cats, birds and doves, herons and grebes, in a host of different positions and in different moments of their normal activities all create this universe of feathers and trills, of extended, variegated wings, of feline grace and of canine faithfulness. A world very close to that of man and deeply moving for those who genuinely love animals.

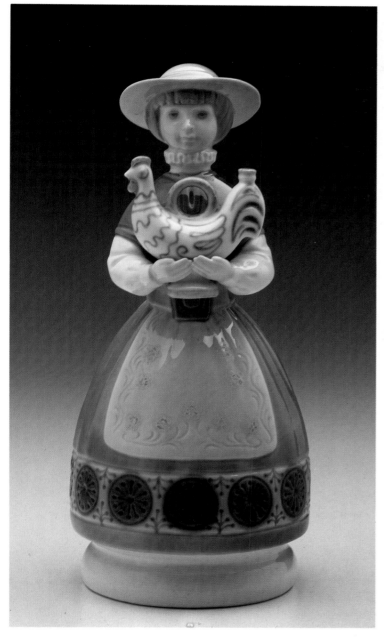

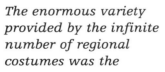

The enormous variety provided by the infinite number of regional costumes was the inspiration for these pretty figurines in which there is a combination of both imaginary and real motifs.

Porcelain pieces depicting fauna are joined by this family of elephants which, sensing danger, flee from the place they had been hitherto.

The *Universe of Stylised Characters* honours one of the most notable characteristics of Lladró porcelain: stylisation. That elongation of figures, reminiscent of the figures that El Greco painted so many years before, has been a fundamental trait of these porcelain pieces almost since they first saw the light of day. A trait that gives them elegance and spirituality, at the same time removing them from any hint of vulgarity that the subject itself may have and conferring upon them the category of work of art and elevating them above what the figure represents. For this reason the figure of the old couple does not express —far from it— the bitter side of decrepitude, but its serene, sweet side. Similarly, the group formed by the poor street musician and the wandering flower seller does not inspire the pity that destitution usually awakens in us, but rather feelings of sympathy and tenderness for simple humblenes and poverty accepted without rancour.

A theme which seems tailor made to be represented in porcelain is that of romanticism. Indeed, in *The Romanticism of Porcelain,* in which the feminine figure dominates throughout, everything seems to come together to create a world of dreams and poetry, from the elegant feminine costumes of the period to the grace of poses and postures, via the delicious evocations of magnificent gardens and flower-covered balustrades. Willows and vines, vases overflowing with flowers, exotic trees, all conspire to evoke the highly romantic, melancholy charm of a bygone age.

The section *Inspiration in Literary Themes* is, to a certain extent, similarly evocative of the past.

Birds lend themselves extraordinarily well to being reproduced in porcelain, perhaps because their outline is so streamlined and their plumage is so beautiful.

Thus this dove which is about to take off from the branch on which it was resting clearly expresses all the tension contained in the movement.

Literature, as has been demonstrated on so many occasions, is an inexhaustible source of subject matter for many artistic manifestations. Porcelain in particular has discovered in literature one of its richest vehicles for expression. The delicacy of the material lends itself admirably to the delicacy of sentiments expressed by so many figures from the world of books. What could better portray the love of Romeo and Juliet than a fragile, subtly coloured piece in porcelain! But the material has also been used to express Hamlet's doubts, Othello's stormy, jealousy-racked love, and the sublime madness of that knight-errant from La Mancha, our immortal Don Quixote.

The religious tradition was also destined to be represented here, in the section entitled *A Serene Devotion* where, in addition to a number of simple, exquisite Nativity scenes, the impressive figure of Santa Teresa stands out alongside the beautiful and highly original figures of the Three Wise Men which the Lladró brothers presented as a gift to Pope Paul VI.

In total contrast to this is the section entitled *An Immortal Heritage: the Genius of the Orient.* What has been said previously about romanticism can equally be applied to these figures representing dancers from Bali or Japanese girls wearing their traditional kimonos since both, in real life, in the flesh, are remarkably similar to porcelain figures. Both are short in stature, slender in figure, of delicate features, silken skinned and of graceful movements and inimitable postures. There is nothing so like porcelain than these tiny, fragile oriental women who have the divine gift of being able to convert each of their movements into

Deep knowledge of the world of the dance and body positions adopted have resulted in the creation of this ballerina (Columbine) who, though in repose, keeps her body taut in an attitude of dynamic expectation.

The total surrender and sacrifice of the nun's calling is superbly expressed in these stylised figures representing silence and mysticism.

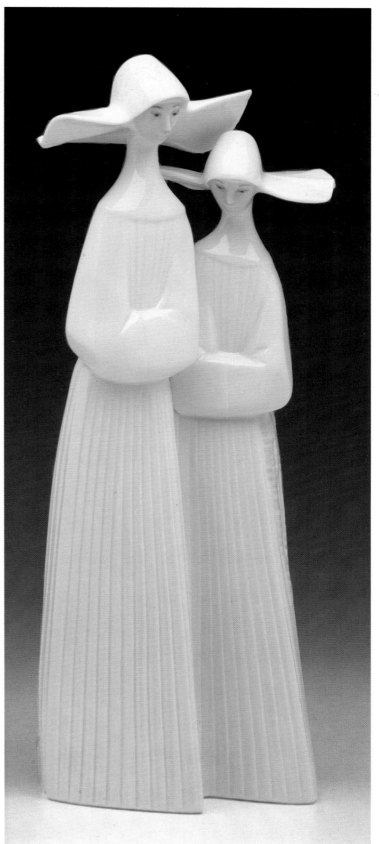

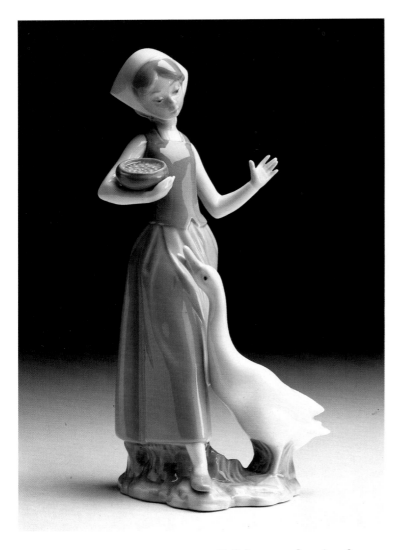

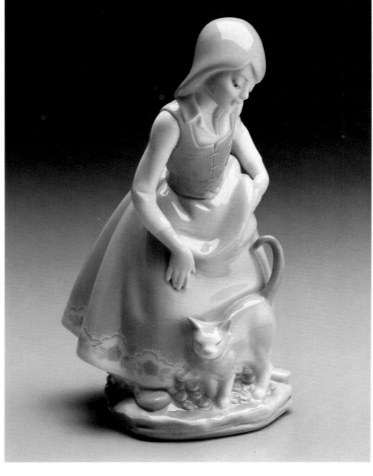

Children and animals are featured widely in Lladró porcelain, often converted into veritable masterpieces with a captivating human warmth. Such is the case of these two little girls, *one of whom shows her surprise at the goose's insistence on being given its share of food, while the other expresses contentment as her cat rubs against her and purrs.*

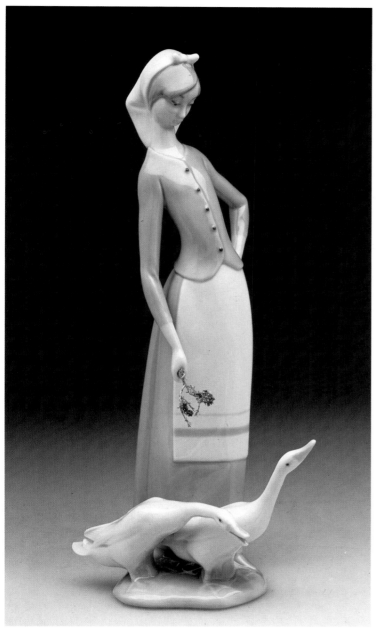

The young peasant girl and her geese form a group evocative of the simplicity of country life. The elongated body of the girl has its counterpart in the upwardly outstretched neck of one of the fowls.

poetry. It was inevitable, therefore, that they should be reproduced in porcelain.

The nude feminine figure was also represented, though discreetly and in a tone that could not possibly offend good taste and decorum. The very title of the section *The Modesty of Nudes,* itself indicates the tact and discretion with which the subject is treated. On the other hand, porcelain is a material that can suggest nothing other than purity and limpidity. Thus the Lladró nudes are neither obscene nor provocative. There is not the slightest emphasis on details, only on the body as a whole in all its harmony and morphological purity, in all its youthful, naïve grace. To achieve this end, many of these figures are without colour, a detail which successfully contributes to giving that note of demureness required. Similarly, some of the figures in question are represented with their eyes closed, as if they were shut inside themselves, indifferent to their surroundings and, above all, preventing the possibility of a glance spoiling the purity of the representation. The group formed by the *Three Graces,* a subject prolifically represented in all arts, is a valid example of this.

Finally, a last group consisting of porcelain pieces which, by their very nature, a section apart from the others: objects which, while still decorative, have an additional utilitarian function. I am referring to the section entitled *Porcelain in the Service of Games and Design* that consists, indeed, of pieces that fulfil these two conditions. What is useful can also be beautiful and must be beautiful whenever possible. A chess set, a series of lamps or flower vases are pieces that fulfil

The author of this enchanting group of six girls arranged as if each one of them were seated at a dressing-table has created a study of coquetry —the eternal, primordial feminine quality— that is both stylised and elegant.

Note the perfect harmony of this group of geese, each one performing a different task characteristic of these birds: while one, highly watchful, has sensed danger, another cleans its plumage, while the third interrupts the same task on hearing the warning cry of its mate.

The curious obtuse-angled position of this youth attempts to suggest repose and dreams, cleary visible in his enraptured expression.

Left: two samples of the perfection with which porcelain in expert hands can reproduce feminine faces, idealising them, and create products in which the practical and the beautiful are joined.

This girl mandolin player is an exquisite figure in which the colour combination conveys a kind of ethereal serenity, transforming her into an allegory of music.

*The group of six little angels reproduced here responds
to the attraction man has always felt towards these
ethereal beings who in religious art have almost
invariably been depicted as children. Here we see them
in a variety of positions playing different musical
instruments.*

The snow-white dove, symbol of peace, is represented in this exquisite group (which in fact is two separate pieces) depicting a pair of these birds. The male fans out its tail to attract the female. The simplicity of the lines enhances the beauty of these winged creatures.

In this other pair, where the birds' heads and necks face each other, their sex can be distinguished above all in the different tail sizes, the feathers of which are treated with singular mastery.

With these tender puppies it is possible to form different groups by placing them in the position most favoured by the owner. The well modelled heads enhance the feeling of affection these little animals produce.

Such a typical farm animal as the hen could not possibly have been omitted from this kind of group, and here she is represented in a number of characteristic postures.

The way this fowl majestically struts about, in its overcoat of feathers, is one of the great achievements by porcelain artists.

admirably this double assignment. The beauty and charm of a vase or a table lamp, whether the latter is in the form of a figure or of a simple base, is something that can be seen in a great many homes. The chess set, with its thirty-two porcelain pieces of six different kinds, is an impressive work of art. On such small figures it was required to reproduce faithfully medieval costumes in every detail. Needless to say, these thirty-two pieces representing warriors and monarchs of the Middle Ages arranged on a shining board, when they are not being used constitute a magnificent showpiece.

With this vast variety of subject-matter, with this impressive baggage of technique and talent, and with this skill in modelling and the use of colour, the moment of plenitude was reached, the years when all the Lladró lines triumphed, years in which apart from creating the astonishing collection we have outlined here, the Lladró brothers also worked in other areas, such as the use of matt paste and sandstone ceramic, with excellent results.

It was towards the end of this period of recent history that two events occurred which were to add even more to an already highly fruitful harvest. One of these was the launching of a series of collections which, by virtue of the limited number and great value of the pieces, immediately acquired great prestige in what was an already highly esteemed overall production. These are the so-called "collections for the elite", "limited series", etc., collections aimed at a smaller, highly demanding clientele in terms of good taste and artistic intuition. And these collections created through a sublimation of what had already

Struggles between wild horses to remain master of a certain territory or to win the affection of a female can occasionally provide highly dramatic moments. One of these disputes has been chosen for one of this pieces, possibly the one in which the impression of movement has been best achieved.

In the oriental style, Hinus stand out by virtue of their serene exoticism, represented in the calm positions adopted by the figures (men and gods) while praying or meditating. The piece represented here is a masterpiece of detail and adornments.

The hieratic position that the human figure sometimes adopts while meditating is momentarily broken here by the artist as from the middle of the torso.

The ballerina reproduced on the right is a display of artistry in that both the sensation of waving movement and of the transparency of the fine cloth covering the lower part of the body, revealing part of the legs, have been achieved.

This robust horse so magnificently harnessed is another masterpiece in which the vigour and power of the animal are combined with perfection of form and harmony in colour.

The easily startled timidity of deer is clearly expressed in this head (next page), in which the intense gaze and the position of the ears show that this animal has seen or heard something alarming which has left it tense and fearful.

The harpist in this figure appears to be drawing a wide circle in the air, and the prolongation of one of the sides of the instrument contributes to this impression. The colour combination once again adds beauty to the piece.

emerged with all the attributes of perfection, naturally aroused the interest of many institutions and many museums.

The second event was the publication of a book, profusely illustrated in full colour, which describes the genesis of the company and its subsequent activities over the years described here as the "most recent history" . The book, in Spanish and English editions, was reprinted nine times and sold over 100,000 copies.

Thus Lladró achieved the consolidation of an artistic style that became accepted and admired all the world over. A period of artistic plenitude was reached with a creative power so fecund that new splendour emerged from the old. Lladró pieces spread further and further afield, crossing seas and oceans and going from one continent to another. Today they are to be found all over the world, after a peaceful conquest, after an invasion with battles of flowers... And like those old colonial empires that brandished swords and placed standards in all latitudes, today the artistic empire of Lladró unfurls the banner of grace, of beauty and of sensitivity in the four corners of the world. For this reason, just as was said in the past about the vast Spanish empire of Philip II, it can be said today that for Lladró the sun never sets.

The Virgin and Child is a piece in which the undoubtedly Gothic tradition of its origin is broken by the expression of the young mother and the upright position of the Child, whose white robes are enhanced by the quilted clothes of the Mother.

This water carrier, who bears a jar precariously balanced on her head, remind us, by virtue of her distinguished demeanour, of the dignity of Egyptian statues.

This pair of eskimo children, wrapped up in their typical, white clothes, are overcome by sleep after a hard day's work.

Porcelain, as we know, originated in the East, and very often returns to its roots, as in these colourful figures which, nevertheless, have been given a western feeling and treatment.

Oriental and classical fantasy gave birth to the centaur, a mythical creature half man and half horse. Here the theme has been given a new treatment in that the centaurs are children, a fact which also permitted greater freedom of expression.

This exquisite duck has been given a plumage copied from reality embellished by a coat of gold varnish.

The goblet represented here is the product of the symbiosis between more or less geometrical forms on the bowl and a classically inspired human figure. Furthermore, the colour combination enhances the formal beauty of the piece.

These Thai dancers are an artistic tour de force in that the complexity of their lavish costumes have been reproduced in minute detail. The positions of the hands and the slant of the bodies contribute towards the impression of movement.

The little girl with her basket full of lovely flowers has sat down to rest, accompanied by her dog. We do not know why she remains so pensive, but we suspect that she imagines she is joining in some game with her schoolfellows.

On the other hand, this young lady who is half lying on her basket of lettuces shows by her expression, lost in the distance, that her body and mind are undergoing those changes that will eventually make her a woman.

This little girl cutting wild flowers in the countryside has had to kneel down in order to cut one which has caught her attention, forcing the artist to give her body a zigzag motion and overcome the difficulties of modelling such a position.

A girl with tresses and with thick clogs on her feet has sat down and placed her basket of fruit at her side. Suddenly she has become transfixed, her eyes stare without seeing and her hand can hardly hold her doll. Everything seems to indicate that puberty is imminent.

The sad, melancholic Harlequin reappears here, except that now he is represented as a child. The girl, dressed like young ladies at the turn of the century, seems to be waiting for someone who does not come. As usual, the colours contribute to the beauty of what is already an exquisite piece.

Children's love for animals is reflected in these two touching works. The girl stroking her dog has her faithful counterpart in the little boy hugging his donkey (Platero?).

"The girl with the sweet tooth" could be the title of this scene of the girl about to share the contents of the honey jar with her faithful companions, her puppies. These anxiously wait to receive their part of the booty, while the expression on the girl's face reflects the thrill of doing something forbidden.

Children and flowers. Both the girl carrying flowers in her skirt and the boy pushing the cart overflowing with flowers of all kinds and colours are extraordinarily attractive pieces with the variegated flowers as their main theme.

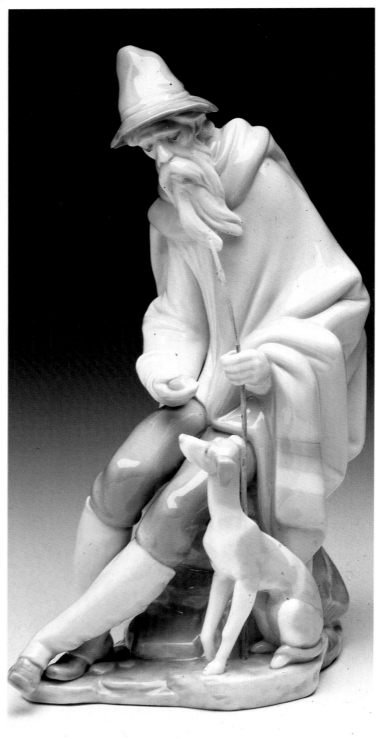

This clown, captured at a dramatic moment during a break in his performance, reveals to us the inner tragedy of a person who has to conceal his own sorrow and melancholy in an effort to make others laugh.

The beggar and his dog, about to share the only crust of bread the former has managed to procure, have been treated in this finely toned piece as a hymn to friendship between the man and his animal companion.

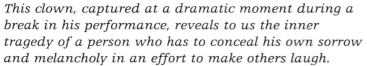

A new image of rest is offered by this little shepherd girl who, with her eyes closed as if overcome by sleep, hugs against her own body that of her favourite lamb.

A FUTURE ALREADY PRESENT

The spirit that informs those who contribute to the creation of these artistic works, Lladró porcelain, can never in its daily tasks consider itself satisfied, so that like the idealist who has set himself an apparently unattainable goal but struggles unceasingly to achieve it, these artists and craftsmen fight a daily battle in which they pose increasingly difficult problems merely for the supreme pleasure of overcoming new difficulties that appear, both in the field of theory and in that of practice, with the aim of producing a work even more exquisite than all those they have produced hitherto, and endowing this work with potential for the future.

This desire always to advance, so visible in these beautiful creations, naturally originates a constant vigilance that leads, often unbeknown to those taking part, to a refined sense of anticipation, a situation that means that, in a very short space of time, when the wide range of possibilities offered by the Lladró organisation is placed at the disposal of the new idea, what seemed to be a project for the future or a possibility that had barely been sketched immediately becomes converted into a present reality.

However, the consolidation of the success that Lladró porcelain enjoys worldwide is by no means the fruit of such rapid execution. This success is due to something much more subtle than anything referring to the creation methods employed; it is due to the intellectual process that has managed to understand and faithfully interpret the most

A magnificent vase in which there is a clear oriental influence.

The attraction aroused by oriental porcelain is reflected in this pair of young Japanese women who, on a tiny artistic bridge, are speaking of the flowers.

The herons represented here enhance the contrast between the verticality of the bird that looks towards the sky with the almost verticality created by the open wings of his companion.

A pair of angel musicians, gently coloured, whose postures enhance the ethereal movements of beings that move among the clouds.

*An artistic group reproducing a form of urban transport
common until very recently in certain oriental towns.
In this case, the coolie has just brought the rickshaw
to a halt and the lady proceeds to close the sunshade that
has protected here during her journey.*

Animals and flowers, two great creations by Porcelanas Lladró, are brought together in these four groups. Anecdotes (particularly that of the cat contemplating the frog) are the pretext here for uniting the forms and colours of animals with all kinds of exquisite flowers.

intimate desires the lovers of these artistic figures that attract by their very intrinsic beauty, and also the capacity to foresee in time the use of canons of beauty that would become fully accepted by the greatest possible number of people, both in the present and in the future.

Thus, by way of example, who could deny that this bride, advancing daintily towards the altar where she will find the love destined to fill her life, is the bride of the future, of future eras, the eternal bride? Will not the cats of the future, just as these in their basket adorned with flowers, look at the world around them with the same astonishment? And what about puppies inspecting the world in which they will have to live? Also the mother ducks of the future will tell their little ones that snails are a genuine delicacy.

Furthermore, it seems highly unlikely that herons, who throughout their daily lives repeat positions and postures inherited from the very origin of the species —postures that acquire a cosmic significance when they become a nupcial dance the sole purpose of which is to ensure the survival of these fine creatures– will abandon their complicated rituals in the future.

Similarly we can ask ourselves if the children of the future will no longer get the same enjoyment out of the merry-go-round, however sophisticated its forms may become, and play upon it with the same gaiety as those of our times.

If, leaving aside purely anecdotical considerations, we consider the processes of manufacture and finish, we shall be forced to reach identical conclusions. Will not the gentle pastel shades delight the eyes of the future as they do those of now? Will not the delicacy of flower petals arouse in people of all eras the same sensation of admiration and beauty? Does not the flight of fantasy that led to the conception of these angels contribute to the present something that belongs to the future? Will not the elegance of the human figure, which far exceeds the embellishment that any kind of attire might give if, whatever care is lavished on the coiffure, whatever jewellery adorns it, continue forever, whatever changes may occur in the meantime? Will not the representation of

embroideries, tulles and lace, although the moment may come when they are very different from those of the present day, require identical solutions in the future?

It is clear, therefore, that if we consider most of the questions posed above, we will have to reply that Lladró, by synthesising essential elements in the figures represented, such as the strength of a horse or the agility and feverish activity of birds, has endowed them with an eternal quality that has converted them into representations of a future that is already with us.

On the other hand, the wide circulation of these porcelain pieces, admired all the world over by members of very different cultures, means similarly that their future course needs no more changes or variations than those occurring normally in the constant evolution of cultured human societies. Moreover, the transmission of the taste for Lladró porcelain from one generation to the next in the same family also corroborates the certainty in the future the pieces now appearing will be recognised as belonging to that family.

The gentle pastel shades of this piece contribute to create the atmosphere of chaste candidness with which the bride advances towards the altar while two bridesmaids hold the train of the dress. A jocular note of humanity is introduced by the fact that one of the girls has been distracted from the ceremony by something that has attracted her attention.

Four little birds have been surprised when they were resting among plants and flowers and the movements they had only just begun have been interrupted. By virtue of their beauty, the flowers in this piece are as much protagonists as the birds themselves.

The famous children's amusement of the merry-go-round has been captured in this figure of a fairground horse mounted by a pretty little girl holding a bunch of flowers in her right hand. The sensation of movement is so great that we expect the horse to rise up at any moment.

This piece, representing two little Valencian children on horseback, could be described as truly remarkable. Our attention is immediately attracted by the fragility of the children and the vigour and power emanating from the sturdy horse. Outstanding here are the filigrees on the girl's dress and the magnificent harnesses of the horse.

The grace and harmony of the twenties is represented in this couple —an ambassador and his wife— in which the artist has devoted considerable time to the lace of the sophisticated dress of the lady and to the gentleman's jacket front. Outstanding here are the harmonious colour combinations.

Elite works

Within the whole range of the highly elaborate works produced by the Lladró family, there is a collection of figures in which the attention lavished on all pieces was increased to the maximum in order to create a selection which, being those most highly esteemed by the Lladró brothers, totally satisfy the tastes of those people who have become refined and highly demanding collectors of these pieces.

It need not be said, either, that even the smallest details have been treated with utmost care in order fully to satisfy the appetites of those who find greatest spiritual solace contemplating the purest beauty and caressing with their eyes the curves, the details and the daring solutions that have been applied to these creations in order to transform them into genuine artistic gems.

This piece narrates one of the culminating moments of the hunt, in which the pack has managed to catch up with the deer that fled terrified from the hounds' teeth and the men's shots. Tension, fear and impotence

predominate the atmosphere of the piece which is a tour de force in dynamism and the capturing of movement, based on the quality of the colouring and the refined, painstaking modelling.

The range of subjects covered by these works for the elite is vast, despite the short period of time that has passed since they were first created, since the intention has been to give visible form in such exquisite material as porcelain to a series of facets capable of satisfying the most varied preferences of those who will possess and contemplate them.

If not a single Lladró piece leaves the factory without first having been examined, analysed and supervised by a team of expert technicians and artists, these Elite works have furthermore been subjected to the strict, constant guardianship of the Lladró brothers themselves, who have taken up as a very special challenge the obtention of works as extraordinary as they are beautiful. Time and time again, therefore, it was necessary to destroy what had been produced in order to alter a small detail, not because it was superfluous or clashed in any way, nor even because it was a mistake, but simply to enhance even more the beauty that could already be perceived in the still unfinished work.

These small vacillations are perfectly understandable, therefore, if one considers, for example, those works which represent hunting scenes, such as the moment when the pack has

The coach (which could be taken from the children's tale of Cinderella) is a prodigious feat of craftsmanship by virtue of the attention given to details not only of modelling, but also to colour, which displays a whole range of subtle shades.

This group of turtle doves has stopped to rest during a journey of migration. Among the branches of a tree they rest and clean their feathers.

The golden eagle, that most majestic of birds, lands beside its nest with a tidbit in its beak for its offspring. Its wings, which have yet to be folded over its body, adopt a heraldic position allowing its wonderful plumage to be seen in detail, enhanced even further by the highlights applied by the artist.

already caught the prey or when the huntsmen on their nervous mounts hurry towards the place where hounds and prey are locked in a struggle to the death, scenes in which the simple movement of a leaf, of a stone or of a body can enhance the tragic sense of the struggle or convert it into a simple posture. The same is true of the variation in the eyes of the observer produced by the subtle change of a single colour.

As regards the subject matter, in the case of children's stories, for example, especial care has been taken to ensure that these tales that open their minds to things so important as fantasy and illusion should also appeal to art lovers; thus a rounded coach, revealing its pumpkin-like origin, welcomes a distressed Cinderella who hears the chimes of midnight that signal the end of the spell and the loss of her fine slipper. In another piece there is a magnificent coach that, drawn by four wonderful horses, carries a couple who seem to belong to the court of a dreamlike country.

The subject of animals, one of the most successful Lladró creations, has not been neglected in this series. The turtle doves, perched on the branches of a tree, that move, bill and coo and clean their plumage, form a dignified, pleasantly coloured piece. Such dignity reaches its zenith in the figure of the nest of the eagle, king of the air, with his powerful, majestic flight, who here has paused in the corner where the nest has been built and where he brings the tidbit for the young bird that will soon inherit the proud kingdom in which other birds will be its vassals. The plumage of this male is so realistic that the bird has become the archetype of this class of animal.

At his side the pair of ducks would be truly magnificent even if we were to overlook the wonderful colours of the male's plumage, something we certainly could never do, since the male has been modelled with such daring that it is impossible to repress the feeling that he is about to land on the water beside his mate at any second.

The figure of the woman could not possibly be forgotten in this Elite collection, in which the theme has been tackled from three angles. In the first of these it could be said that fragile femininity has been reproduced, the somewhat literary fragility of XIXth-century ladies who needed constant protection on the part both of mother and father, and whose only mission in life was to show off magnificent dresses that enhanced their undeniable beauty. Thus we see them in this attractive group formed by there young ladies in their sumptuous clothes and their small parasols

This other coach, pulled by four finely harnessed horses, is a typically rococo vehicle with its haughty driver and spruce lackeys. Outstanding here are the minute decoration of the wheels, sides and roof of the coach.

Three little nineteenth-century ladies pause suddenly before something which has caught their attention on the ground. The suddenness of this act has caused their dresses to stir, which the artist has captured in a wave of folds and lace which delights the eye.

This group of Valencian women is one of the best examples of the Lladró artists' skill in the difficult task of representing textiles, cloth and lace, and baskets of flowers.

Hunters after the fox ride furiously with their pack in pursuit of their catch. Steeds that have just jumped over an obstacle and hounds all adopt positions indicative of maximum effort; the men, also tense and agitated, sport their typical hunting costumes.

This magnificent Lladró porcelain piece is one of their most interesting for a number of reasons. The audacious position of the male, about to land on the water, is truly remarkable, since it is joined to the plant only by the back part of the body.

The Venetian gondola,
with its nineteenth-
century characters
aboard, is one of the
great creations of Lladró,
by virtue both of the
carefully created
atmosphere and of the
attention paid to the
smallest details.

A tiny Harlequin drives an equally tiny horn of plenty pulled by a silky donkey. From the horn protrudes a host of flowers whose display of colours will light up the whole world.

(a tour de force on the part of the artists) who seem to be amusing themselves observing the antics of a tiny puppy. Let us not be deceived, however. If the moment were to arrive, this fragility, this costly attire, these daring coiffures and these rich jewels that now adorn them would be replaced in an instant and these weak, graceful young ladies would become the strong woman of the Bible.

Another angle is represented by three little Valencian women offering flowers to the Virgin. This masterly piece contains details that make it one of the most successful groups in the whole of the Elite series. For instance, the regional costumes, besides being ones in which popular fantasy ran riot, making them among the most sumptuous of the many found in Spain, contain such a quantiy of embroidery that they become truly unique; however, to this must be added the almost tactile softness of the bodices and white *mantillas*. Furthermore, there is the basket of flowers that the girls are undoubtedly offering to the *Virgen de los Desamparados*, Patron Saint of Valencia. Each petal of each these roses is such a marvel of execution and colouring that, on being combined together to form the flower, they create a prodigy that surpasses even nature herself. The group creates such an aura of fascination that one can almost smell the subtle perfume of the roses.

Finally we see the group of Japanese musicians. If in the full education of any person music must play a prominent role, in the case of Oriental women in general, and Japanese women in particular, it was an essential subject since it was used to accompany song, dance and recitation, as well as to provide group amusement in the form of small orchestras. And if the girl in question was a *geisha,* music became absolutely indispensable. In this group, the reproduction of the instruments, from the strings of which tones and chords are obtained that are unfamiliar to western ears, has been painstakingly carried out so that their exotic forms will act as a counterbalance to the magnificent costumes of the musicians. Beauty, fascination and harmony could be the nexus that acts as an intimate link between these feminine groups that are apparently so different.

On the other hand, one of the many manifestations that romanticism can adopt is that of the incomparable atmosphere of the city of Venice, with her baroque buildings, the highly colourful world of her painters and the magic of her canals, represented in the mind's eye by these typical vessels, the gondolas, in which musicians and finely voiced gondoliers play pieces and sing songs that delight the ear of those on board. The excellent *La Gondola* (the gondola) piece reproduces this feeling and the boat, as if its maker had a horror of empty spaces, has been decorated with carvings that intertwine and cover the sides of the boat with complicated designs. The passenger, an exquisite lady who fans herself to obtain relief from the heat of summer, listens enraptured by the music (a piece by Vivaldi perhaps?) that her two admirers dedicated to her. Behind, standing on a sumptuous rug, two gondoliers, untouched by the charms of the music and intent only upon their mission, guide the beautiful vessel on its course through the fantasies of the imagination.

Among the creations that have made Lladró so celebrated, three in particular stand out: flowers, children and animals. It need not surprise us, therefore, that in these Elite series a group has been created in which all three are brought together to be contemplated at the same time. As usual the extraordinary quality of flowers has been faithfully reproduced, with their silky petals and erect stems, emerging from an unusual cart which we might say was the horn of floral plenty, since here classical mythology has been transformed in such a way that from its heart the only wealth that issues forth is the beauty of flowers. The driver of the cart is one of the typical Lladró creations based on the Italian *Commedia,* while it is pulled by a silk skinned donkey that could almost be *Platero* revived to pull, harnessed by a chain of flowers, an imaginary cart full of floral fantasies.

The Card Players is a highly intricate group based on Spanish literature of the Golden Age, in which soldiers travelled and lived from one inn or tavern to another. In order to obtain it, it was necessary to make a careful study of the customs and attire of XVIIth-century soldiers. The positions and poses in particular have been very closely analysed, especially that of the player who has to make the last bid and who is the personification of doubt, since on his decision depends whether he will be the winner or the loser. The details of the wine jugs, the swords, the cards and the coins are all the result of painstaking study.

However, not everything in life is merrymaking and leisure. There is also struggle, sacrifice and risk. And the fisherman, so often told how expensive his catch is, must wage an eternal battle against waters that, while providing him with a living, may also be the cause of his death. This, therefore is the theme of another Elite piece: the rude struggle between men and the waves. The tension of the helmsman, guiding the boat on the course that will lead to their salvation, contrasts with the affectionate concern of the little boy who, sitting in the bows, and feeling beneath his feet the shudders of the boat as it is hit time and again by the violent sea, hugs his dog in a subconscious desire to same him and save himself.

Card players belong to one of those reconstructions of seventeenth-century life based not only on narratives by contemporary writers but also on literary recreations by romantic writers of the XIXth century.

This piece could be described as a genuine masterpiece, in which every detail suggests the never ending struggle between sailors and the sea.

In this group of Japanese women musicians (next page), two of them, seated play their stringed instruments while the third, standing, sings the poem she holds in her hand.

A collector's world

Evidently we are not now going to analyse here what collecting is, that kind of ancestral desire to keep things or objects that attract, either by virtue of their beauty or of the enormous difficulty that finding them represents.

Although we must accept that beauty is subjective and that each individual chooses items for his collection according to criteria that are absolutely personal, it is nevertheless true that the attraction that most people feel towards Lladró porcelain can be divided into two main types: that corresponding to those who like all the pieces, irrespective of classes or categories, and that corresponding to those whose preferences lead them to choose one of the facets that are represented in these porcelain figures.

Bearing in mind this second category of collectors, since those of the first are satisfied by the variety of these porcelains, Lladró has considered it expedient to concentrate on certain themes which, by virtue of the special circumstances that have brought about their success, have led to the existence of collectors specialising in one or other of them.

These themes are by no means highly sophisticated; on the contrary, they are those deeply rooted in human sentiment and affection. Based, therefore, on the foregoing premises, a series of figures has been produced each component of which, though a work of art in its own right that would grace any collection, combines with its fellows to form a group which, taking an analogy from music, could be considered theme and variations. In this way, the number of different figures expressing the same theme can be increased until an attractive group is formed of exquisite pieces in accordance with the personal tastes of the collector.

Outstanding among the themes that go to form these groups is that of the clown, those essential figures of the great show that is the circus which strongly attract our sympathy by virtue of their double personality. On the one hand, the face we all see, that of extroversion and joy, the creator of situations that cause hilarity among those who observe their antics; on the other, the hidden face, that of the person who is forced to make others laugh regardless of what he may be suffering inside, in his innermost being, which on occasions may be a genuine tragedy which must nevertheless be overcome. In this sense, the pieces that show them after their performance has ended are true masterpieces.

There is another aspect to this world, however; namely that of the boy clowns, who really are always cheerful and playful, who have fun with puppies and ball games and who can even make

The ikebana artist is a piece that contains such a high poetical note that it is an extraordinary work of art.

music. The acquisition of different figures of this type can lead to a most attractive collection with a wide variety of poses, postures and colours.

The Orient, the origin, as we have said so many times, of porcelain, is another of the themes for collections easy to cultivate. Indeed, the exquisite coiffures, the magnificent kimonos and the studied postures of the highly refined Japanese courtesy combine to form a series of figures to which new ones can always be added and in which these same postures, such as those dedicated to flower arranging, *ikebana* or the harmonious arrangement of these on branches, have been analysed and crystallised in a new, different position. We can cite by way of examples the five little Japanese girls caressing flowers, the *ikebana* artist the young dancers with their fans and sunshades, and those who adopt the postures characteristic of their refined education.

Worthy of special mention are the Nativity Scenes or *Belenes,* groups formed from figures so dear both to Spanish and South American people. Popular in origin, and generally of clay, the arrival on this earth of the Child Jesus was celebrated with the reproduction of a simple manger where, in the heat given off by the bodies of an ox and a mule, the Child Jesus lay resting on the ground together with his parents, Joseph and Mary. Later, the number of participants increased astonishingly: shepherds, animals, angels, Wise Men, etc. Therefore Lladró decided to create the original nucleus of Saint Joseph, the Virgin and the Child, around which can be added —or it might be better to say collected— the figures of the Wise Men offering their gifts to Jesus as well as other figures

whose number may increase in successive stages.

Another theme worthy of special mention is that of the Valencian children (*huertanitos* and *huertanitas*) figures which, whether collected to form a group or not, each have their own intrinsic beauty and for the creation of which careful studies of child psychology were carried out. To this was added an extraordinary richness of attire and, though it need not be said, in the furnishing, since the chairs in which the little girls rest are of an almost unsurpassable beauty. Equally exquisite are the bouquets of flowers in their hands, one of the most genuine successes of Lladró porcelain. The little Valencian boys, with their amusing grimaces, are of the same beauty as these other figures.

This Holy Family, in which several characteristics of Lladró porcelain are combined, corresponds to the Nativity Scenes by these artists, stemming from a long tradition in Spain. The elongated yet robust figure of Joseph is an outstanding element here.

These child clowns reveal that, despite being clowns, they continue to be children; it should not surprise us, therefore, that they like toys and dogs. This group consists of three loose figures, each of which is a genuine work of art.

In these magnificent pieces the clowns' expressions are analysed, not when they are making the audience laugh but rather, once they are on their own, when they can express how they really are and give vent to their inner feelings. Their expressions, between sorrowful and nostalgic, show us something of their real personality.

The group formed by these five little Japanese girls constitutes a study both of the different positions adopted by the human body and the feelings towards plants and flowers felt by that people. Indeed, cach of the girls caresses a flower with her hand.

The Christmas custom of making Nativity Scenes is a deep rooted tradition in Spain and in Latin America. The figurines composing them, by means of which we remember the birth of Christ and his adoration by shepherds and the Three Wise Men, when they are modelled by the artists of Lladró acquire an artistic value that transforms them into truly admirable pieces.

An exquisite group representing four girls adopting the postures of Japanese dances and greetings, which have been studied in every detail in order to reproduce the movements of the oriental body. In order to enhance the sensation of movement, parasols and fans were included.

This group of four pieces (next page), reproducing four young Valencian girls dressed in regional costume, is a delicious study of girls taking part in some flowers offering. The tension of waiting has made them abandon somewhat their initial composure.

A group of boy gardeners whose body positions reveals their different relationships with the flowers. Thus, while the one in the middle carries his flowers in a basket, the second seems to have given up waiting for the person to come and take them from him, while the third, tired of waiting, has fallen asleep.

These little musical angels (next page, top), playful and mischievous, are direct descendants of the famous putti which were used during the Italian baroque to decorate altarpieces.

These little girls preparing for bed have been represented already with their nightgowns on. The study of infantile positions reveals perfect observation talents and great delicacy on the part of the artist.

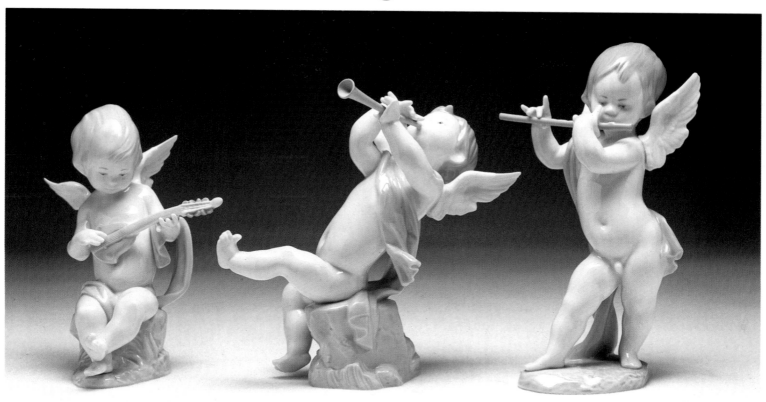

Among other groups there are those formed by angel musicians, representations which originate directly —though given here a more natural, modern treatment— from those marvellous angels which so magnificently adorn baroque altarpieces.

Children about to go to bed, putting on the nightgown that is to be the companion of their dreams, constitute a wide repertoire of figures that can be combined in a variety of ways to produce different groups. The fine irony that can be detected in some of their postures reveals a notable gift of observation regarding the world of children.

The series of little eskimo girls, with its own brand of exoticism, is a marvel of colouration by virtue of the rich, warm clothing that protects them from the freezing conditions in which they live. Outstanding here is the figure of the little girl who with her gloved hand rubs her frozen foot in order to bring it back to life.

At the risk seeming repetitive, we shall say once again that each of the figures forming this series, though they were designed to allow collectors to put together a private world where they feel at home and can enjoy contemplating each of the members, so to speak, of the same family, are sufficiently beautiful and decorative in their own right to be acquired and enjoyed as individuals.

*The terrible cold of the frozen wasteland where eskimos
are forced to live is represented here in the form of
these four girls who, numb with cold, attempt to cover
as much of their bodies as possible.*

Limited issue works

Some creations by Porcelanas Lladró, either by virtue of their subject matter, or because they were so difficult to make, have been produced in series with a limited number of pieces. Most works had enormous acceptance since their subject or the characters represented appeal to a wide range of tastes, so that they are featured as decorative elements in many homes. Others, on the other hand, such as those we are about to examine, require greater discernment on the part of purchasers since their special characteristics also need, at times, a special setting. Indeed, acquiring the figure of a fine bird or a magnificent feline or a beautiful girl, however exquisite and perfect these may be, is not the same as acquiring that of major figures from history or literature, such as that so Spanish of characters, Don Quixote, or Shakespeare's Hamlet. Those who buy these sculptures are undoubtedly people who feel admiration for these figures, and for this reason they give them all the importance they deserve, appreciate them in all their dimensions and display them in their rightful place.

It is to this kind of work that the special treatment to which we referred has been given: an exceptional attention to subject matter, an artistic supervision carried to painstaking extremes, limitation of series and numeration of figures. For, in effect, all the pieces that constitute this limited issues have been duly numbered, a fact which, without the shadow of a doubt, represents the most forceful confirmation of the exceptional prestige they enjoy. Every numbered piece instantly acquires an automatic value and an exclusive character, above all for collectors, since, generally speaking, this little number of pieces is such to the point that, in a way, they can be considered unique. Furthermore, the moulds for these privileged models is destroyed when the number of pieces designated to the series has been reached, so that such figures immediately acquire the category of "unrepeatable works", which supposes that their value rises to the maximum and that interest in them rapidly grows. Given this, the collector must make haste in order to acquire the piece in which he is interested, since once the mould has been destroyed it will never again be made and it will be extremely difficult, not to say impossible, to have the good fortune to come across another one like it. None of the pieces on these pages can ever be produced again.

Naturally enough, all these circumstances together mean that it is a privilege to be the proud possessor of one of these pieces since not only are they very rare but also, and this must be said, the

Yet another version of the knight of the melancholy countenance, Alonso Quijano (Don Quixote).

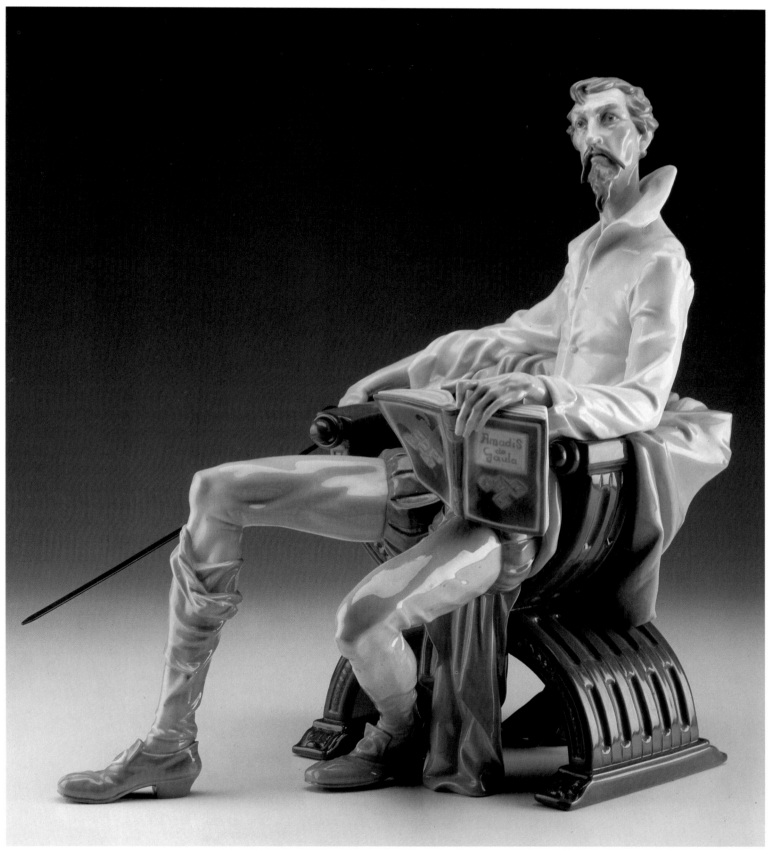

Literature reflected in porcelain has one of its finest manifestations in the scene where Hamlet contemplates Yorick's skull. The contained tension that perturbs the prince's spirit is reflected in his face and in the unfathomable depths of his gaze.

Mistiness and a dream-like quality are the main motifs of this piece, in which the waving feminine bodies and the wide veil become, because of the presence of the doves, a very special allegory of peace.

most refined product by Porcelanas Lladró. And this is true because over and above the already well-known merit and beauty that these pieces possess, those of this particular group are the product of a deliberate search for the most difficult technical and artistic processes possible in this kind of work. Indeed, to the characteristic perfection of Lladró creations has been added a challenge that it seemed impossible to meet: that of expressing in a face of porcelain the inner life of a character and overcoming technical difficulties regarding the balance of elements and the minute attention to detail, problems whose successful solution causes genuine amazement and admiration.

Is not the expression of this Don Quixote truly admirable, in which he clearly tells us that the phrase he has just read has reached the very depths of his soul? If he said so in words it could not be more expressive. The knight has been depicted at a crucial moment of his life, on the threshold of his own insanity. In the sculpture there is no reproduction of any of the celebrated episodes that take place in the book that recounts his adventures; on the contrary, the character has been placed in the first stages of his delirium,

In this representation of a delicate feminine body, the intention of the artist is that the observer should fix his attention on the body itself; for this reason the body is colourless and stands out against its background.

when incessant reading of novels of chivalry peopled his mind with fantasies and launched him, when he finally became completely mad, upon the magnificent folly that was to immortalise him. The face of the famous *hidalgo* is a genuine psychological study in porcelain: his head, suddenly raised, is turned to one side, as if in search of an explanation of what he has just read. And his gaze seems to penetrate into the farthest distance, crossing the regions of his world of hallucinations, further and further removed from reality. His gaze is a mixture of surprise, questioning, and delirium.

The gaunt face and the bony hand in which he holds a copy of *Amadís of Gaul*, in combination with the shabbiness of his attire, complete the image of the gentleman who, —naturally— holds in one had his naked sword, the symbol of the great adventures he is already living in his mind.

Another character who was equally difficult to portray is Hamlet, the unfortunate prince of Denmark from Shakespeare's famous tragedy. As in the previous case, here also the inner drama of the character had to be expressed in porcelain, and this is achieved here not only in the facial expression but also in the posture of the body.

This group of three nubile girls around a tree trunk is an acute analysis of the classical group of the Three Graces, in which a different perspective of the human body has been searched for based on the different position of the arms. The trunk and the bodies have also been contrasted by eliminating the colour from the former.

A coach drawn by a sturdy charger, at the time when the motor car was still to find its place in society, takes two noble ladies and their greyhound for a spin. The technical difficulties (wheels, parasol, etc.), are evident, but despite them, the result is superb.

This pair of dancers represents the spiritual rapture which music and its corporal interpretation produces in those who practise classical, and essentially romantic, dance. The look and the slight approach of the bodies, and the hands that almost touch are still further evidence of the artist's mastery, whose work is embellished with truly masterful nuances.

In this representation of a water carrier a highly characteristic position of the feminine body has been captured when, jutting out her hip, she rest upon it the burden she has to carry. The strong colours contribute to enhance the strength of this young woman.

Porcelain can also used to represent contemporary figures, not just archetypes or people from history. Such is the case of this representation of Queen Elisabeth II of England, dressed in a riding habit.

The hunt is one of the subjects most suitable for representation in porcelain, by virtue not only of the variety of components and the opportunity to reproduce the colourful habits of the huntsmen, but also of the animals that take part in this activity.

However, contrary to the case of Don Quixote, the eyes of this Hamlet in a strangely paradoxical way seem to be looking "inwards" rather than outwards; his gaze does not search for distant horizons but inner abysses and experiences of a recent, bitter past. And this intense melancholy, which both past and present have marked on the face of this unlucky prince and which is so magnificently expressed in this figure, is reinforced by the posture of forlornness and exhaustion of the body. Hamlet's posture does not give the impression that the prince has sat placidly down upon the stone bench; on the contrary, he seems to have fallen infinitely exhausted upon it in a mood of deep and painful dejection. His outstretched left leg gives the impression, indeed, that he has collapsed on the bench, as does the slight forward stoop of the body, which is a typical posture of dejection. In one hand he holds Yorick's skull, whose contemplation should arouse so many wonderful memories. This hand, however, rather than holding the human skull seems to be caressing it.

Many other historic and literary figures are also featured in this exceptional series. A sensational Christopher Columbus, taking possession of the New World, has about it a truly imposing solemnity. A cynical and gouty figure of Henry VIII of England could almost be that monarch himself, while the image of Napoleon, as authoritarian as he was hard-working, is most impressive. And so that not all these figures should be personalities from the past, there is also a delightful representation of Queen Elisabeth II of Great Britain mounted on a horse.

Another display of skill of which the figures in this series can be justly proud is that represented by the pieces Allegory of Peace and Landau Drive, both of which can never be repeated. In this case, the Lladró artists were faced with challenges of technical virtuosity, because the Allegory of Peace is a veritable technical tour de force. The body of the woman, dressed in a light tunic, creates the sensation of ethereal dreamlike scenes, almost of weightlessness, enhanced by the ripple of the wide veil she holds and which we imagine to be moved by a clean, warm wind. The doves, as white as the rest of the composition, complement this symbol of peace, and the fact that they are sustained by the minimum number of support points is a master feat of equilibrium that can only be achieved by Lladró craftsmen.

The representation of the Landau Drive is also a masterpiece whose technical difficulties, such as the ladies' parasols, the wheels of the carriage and other details, can only be overcome by means of absolute mastery of this art. The same mastery can also be seen in a host of other compositions, such as the pair of dancers who join and harmonise their bodies without actually touching, the feminine nudes, chaste and full of naïve grace, or the groups of lively animals or multicoloured floral compositions.

And thus, without making distinctions or giving prominence to one piece over another, it is possible to describe the merits, the beauty, the excelling and the exquisiteness of each and every one of these exceptional figures which undoubtedly constitute the most attractive collection of all Lladró creations.

Sculptural works

It is possible that some people will think that the sculptures featured on these pages are a departure from the kind of Lladró porcelains they are accustomed to seeing and admiring. They may think that Lladró has set out upon a new artistic path, something which, on the other hand, many firms do. This is not the case, however. Though the desire to find new directions is a highly positive, laudable action, in this case the apparently new line which seems to have been adopted is in fact a renewed or recovered line which has direct links to the very beginnings of Lladró porcelain.

Nevertheless, they can be considered a new incursion into the world of art since they contain details and characteristics (of production, materials and artists) which *are* new, though their essence, we insist, is deeply rooted in the years when Lladró was searching for its own, personal style.

This return to the past, or rather this bringing to the present what was past, has its motivations and support which have simultaneously culminated in a new manifestation which we might call "pure sculpture".

Such motivation received its support from the astonishing facility with which the artists employed in the Lladró workshops managed effortlessly to adapt to this kind of "return style", a style which many of them had not had occasion to know. These sculptors, working exclusively for Lladró, successfully adopted new approaches and new methods. The results can be appreciated on these pages, which constitute a veritable parade of the best of these single-colour pieces (so different from those pieces so subtly coloured) and made with a variant of the material used hitherto. Indeed, traditional porcelain posed certain problems when it came to producing these works, which made the artists turn to such variants, much more suitable since to a certain extent they are reminiscent of granite, marble and other materials characteristic of great sculpture. Similarly, these pieces are much larger than those produced so far, yet another characteristic that brings them closer to the traditional concept of sculpture. For their part, the Lladró artists, always under the decisive supervision of the Lladró brothers but nevertheless conserving their own artistic personalities, managed to bring this new, graceful vessel safely to port after it had been launched with such enthusiasm into the seas of art.

The figure entitled *Victory* immediately attracts the attention. The expressive force of this sculpture is enhanced by the position of the head and in the forward thrust of the body. There are no arms or legs, but neither are they necessary. The torso and the head reveal all the determination, express all the overwhelming force of a being, of an idea, of a potential that, in a

This "Victory", by the artist José Puche, is one of the most impressive creations among Lladró porcelain sculptures.

"Prize Fighter", by Salvador Furió, is a sculpture in ceramic that expresses, even without a head and only through the position of the torso and the arms, the state of relaxation after the supreme effort of a bout.

"Brother-in-Arms", by Fernández-Sáez, is a work which expresses both the vigour and the effort necessary to give aid to the wounded soldier. The robust, sturdy figures reflect vast knowledge about the treatment of volumes on the part of the artist.

"In the Distance" is a creation by the artist Salvador Debón of a rare quality: he expresses his highly personal vision of reality by half twisting the body and giving both halves different volumes.

"Bather", by Juan Huerta, shows us a girl emerging from the sea after a swim and about to dry herself with the towel in her hands. This piece has a certain renaissance quality about it.

triumphant manner, opens a way and prepares to sweep away all obstacles.

The work entitled *Brothers-in-Arms* is a fine composition with two protagonists, one of whom is helping the other, in which the sensation of strength —or rather, of effort— that issues from one is contrasted in the extreme exhaustion and defenselessness of the other, who seems to be very badly wounded.

The sculpture entitled *In the Distance* is a delightful work in which a naked, half-kneeling girl turns her head to one side and gazes at something that appears to be in the distance and which has awakened her interest. Not only the position of her head but also the slight, almost imperceptible twist of her body in the same direction and the foreshortening of her left arm thrown backwards also enhance this sudden curiosity which has caused the girl to focus so much attention on a point in the distance.

The sculpture entitled *Bather* is a departure from the usual canons applied in representing this kind of subject. The feminine figure is seen emerging from the water but her demeanour is totally natural, at a far remove from the host of sophisticated bathers that have abounded in painting and sculpture. The woman's hair, and the peculiar, scarcely perceptible sheen on her body suggests that she is still wet, and about to dry herself with the towel she is holding.

The work entitled *Prize-Fighter* is particularly interesting, as it immediately recalls some of the fine statues of the Renaissance. In the same way as the one entitled *Victory* has no arms or legs, this one has no head, because it was unnecessary. All the expressiveness is concentrated in the athletic body, which appears to be sweating, and in the arms, in the relaxed position of a fighter gathering strength between rounds.

All these works, though different from previous ones, continue to have that unmistakeable pulse that one feels in every creation be Lladró which, be they coloured or not, be they large or small, in porcelain or any other material, all seem to have been born from the palpitating soul of their creators. The subject matter in each case is pleasing, emphasizing gentleness and tenderness and fleeing from any hint of unpleasantness or bitterness.

Great masters of sculpture

The most far-reaching step that Lladró has taken, however, has been to begin —and this really *can* be called a new line— a new phase of production in close contact and collaboration with a world-famous artist: the sculptor Pablo Serrano.

It sometimes happens that certain sculptors, rich in art and inspiration, who work with materials characteristic of traditional sculpture, come across technical difficulties when it comes to turning their sculptural dreams into reality. For this reason they have to turn to another artist or groups of artists who, with the proper means and mastery of special techniques, by joining forces make it possible to create this dreamed-of work, as yet without life but which already lives in the fertile realms of thought.

And which artists could better fulfil this purpose than the Lladró brothers? In was they, naturally, who accepted the challenge of this competition, since it really was a competitive challenge that was accepted and met. Lladró made contact with Pablo Serrano and the latter with the great artistic complex which was beginning the search for ways to give modern sculpture another dimension and a new means of expression. Thus took place the meeting of two spirits —which perhaps unbeknown to them were already following parallel paths—, two artistic ideas, two great creative interests: the Lladró brothers expanding and enriching their work without renouncing in any way their solid, well deserved identity; and Pablo Serrano, now able to dispose of the great technical resources at the Lladró plant. Thus porcelain or sandstone clay pieces, the work of Pablo Serrano, came alive in a series controlled and numbered by the artist himself.

This artist was born in Crevillente, Teruel, in 1910. At the age of 18, having studied in Saragossa and Barcelona, he began to work as a sculptor. Later he spent 24 years in Uruguay. He returned to Spain with a certain reputation as an abstract sculptor and obtained the First Sculpture Prize at the II Hispano-American Biennial. He travelled all over Europe and, as from 1957, began to exhibit, to the acclaim both of public and critics, in the main cities of Spain and the rest of Europe. In 1960 he did the same in New York and then in many other places in North America. He was commissioned statues of famous Spanish figures, such as Unamuno, Machado, Isabel the Catholic, etc. Several works by this sculptor, who died recently, are on display in major museums in Europe and America.

This, then, was the man with whom the Lladró brothers established an artists' pact which became a revolutionary event without precedent in the art of porcelain. We are referring to the aforementioned creation of numbered ceramic series, that form of traditional sculpture which, without losing any of its aesthetic and artistic values, could now be reproduced in porcelain, a facet that had hitherto been either considered impossible or prohibitive: that of being produced in a determined number of pieces, generally few, suitably numbered and guaranteed.

The impressive head of Don Quixote on the next page is the most eloquent manifestation of the success and quality of this system. The knight-errant's features bear all the characteristic marks of a work of personal creation and the stamp of the hands that gave them life. And this imprint that Pablo Serrano was to leave, each of the impressions his fingers left in the mass, each furrow and each wrinkle he immortalised in this deluded, tormented face have remained intact in fragile porcelain, with a vigour and an expressive capacity that seem more characteristic of marble or granite than of such a delicate material.

Without ever departing from traditional directions, this new creative phase opens new paths in the career of Lladró, paths which, though fed by the same ideals, will lead to wider objectives. Two branches of art have come together and begun a long journey together.

And the first fruits are already here.

Outstanding among the creations by Pablo Serrano for series of ceramic sculptures, is this "Dynamic Interpretation of the Portrait of Don Quixote", in which the knight-errant's face is elongated by the sytlised beard and the barber's bowl —not helmet— gives him an air of saintliness.

"Caprichos" in porcelain

Pottery has flourished worldwide from the prehistoric age for the making of statuettes of gods and animals. This was due to the high availability of clay in the soil. Compared to marble and bronze, clay had plasticity, which made forming easy. However, many of these terra-cotta statuettes from the primitive and prehistoric eras have religious and sorcery-related meanings. However, even in the classical age, statuettes expressed deep human emotions and movements, typically seen in Tanagra and Myrina figurines. Such traditional expressions of beauty were revived during the 18th century in Meissen, and in Valencia, traditional pottery place in Spain since the 15th century, in the mid 20th century by the Lladró brothers. Characteristics of their small pieces of porcelain, for example, are diversity of motifs, forms with movement, elegant lines, delicate expressions of lace design, and warm tones of pastel colors. In these pieces of porcelain dreams, fantasy, purity and joy are expressed. The maintenance of harmony of such characteristics creates a lovely world of beauty.

To Japanese ceramic lovers, European ceramic art seems similar to their sculptures and paintings in its essence. In Japan, pottery is highly appreciated in the forms of jars, vases, "sake" cups, bowls, and plates. Therefore, with the exception of those made in the prehistoric era for religious purposes, clay pottery in the form of statuettes has rarely been made. This is because the traditional Japanese mentality of beauty favors simplicity compared to that of Europe. This is also seen in Japanese paintings, which are flat and linear. On

The head of a beautiful woman. The delicate techniques which do not allow compromise of the craftsman is impressive.

A flower ornament was the first porcelain piece that Lladró made. Patience is required for such a masterpiece where petals are made separately and combined to make a flower.

An ornament of lace with three roses. Lace is often used as a favorite of Lladró's unique porcelain motif, who seeks feminine, sensitive, gentle, and graceful qualities in lace. Careful attention must be paid not to break the lace. Lace is the magic of porcelain art.

Placing flowers over a piece of lace spread in a basket with a handle. The left basket has roses; the right, daisies. With the pink roses, there is a white piece of lace; with the white daisies, a pink piece of lace.

the contrary, the Japanese dislike strongly artistic designs. In European museums and among European collections of Japanese pottery, there are many multicolored picture plates. This is because polychrome Imari porcelain, which was originally made to be exported to Europe from the late 17th century to 19th century, suited the artistic taste of Europeans rather than that of the Japanese.

However, in Europe, along with pottery for practical purposes, such as plates, jars and bowls, potters created splendid figures of humans, animals and birds as styles of formative art. This opened a world of diversity in art. Such works of art were diverse in style: for example, no glazing in order to enhance the original beauty of the soil terra-cotta, partial coloring of terra-cotta, plaster with only one coat of glaze, multicolored drawings on the piece, etc. When Lladró started pottery, in the fifties, they made more pottery of practical usage; however, in the following years, they concentrated on porcelain sculpture only. This shows the revival of the traditional, formative art and the creation of a new form of art based on the traditional style, besides the making of pottery for pragmatic purposes.

Placing three dahlias over a piece of lace widely spread in a basket. Much effort and time is necessary not only to make the big meshes of the basket, but also combining the tiny petals of the dahlia from the inside, which are over 20 in number. This shows the patience of the craftsman.

The masterpiece of the flower series. A gorgeous jewelry box filled with flowers. Spread over a white piece of lace there are purple bellflowers, pink dahlias, and yellow roses. This jewelry box could be a metaphor of the love of flowers of the people of Valencia.

The characteristics of Lladró porcelains

The characteristics and attractiveness of Lladró's small pieces of porcelain art is, first of all, the diversity of motifs. Here, the motifs are scenes of everyday life, such as ballerinas, men and women, children at play, sports, dancing, and labor, as well as objects such as imaginary animals of classical myths, angels, animals, birds, trees and flowers, hats, and ballet shoes. Such diversity creates a small universe of beauty. However, not only is the diversity of motifs reflected in the art of the small sculptures, but also the inner feelings of these figures are expressed. In these figurines inner feelings such as love, innocence, joy, purity, faith and dreams are expressed and visualized through their expressions and movements.

Another element that directly explains the characteristics of Lladró's small art is the thin and delicate designs of the figures, as seen in the ballerina series, men and woman with hats, lovers, and hunters. Their unusually thin and delicate structures, however, mysteriously enhance a poetic, fantastic and elegant impression through their figures. This is one of the reasons that Lladró's statuettes are loved by many people worldwide.

Lladró's colors become creative and unique. They remind us of Royal Copenhagen porcelain statuettes which have a semi-grayish blue and brown color. But, if they are compared closely, the difference is obvious. The colors of Royal Copenhagen's represent the colors of the sky and North Sea, which consciously express the natural color of Northern Europe. However, Lladró's warm blue and brown colors are those artificially made by an artist. Therefore, the blue in Lladró's pieces are not soft nor dull. It is said that Lladró has over 5,000 color samples; almost only neutral pastels are used. Like in the masterpieces of Q. de La Tour and E. Degas, pastels enhance a high quality color different from those of oil-color and water-color paintings. They are not dull and express a softness and gentleness in the tone of color. The reason Lladró uses in many pieces of work such colors are none other than that the tone of colors in the porcelain statues enhance a poetic atmosphere.

Another attractive feature of Lladró's porcelains is their refined final touch. In the ballerina, and the football players and hunters, the figurines are made up of over ten plaster casts. Then, the joints are connected, with the surface polished and smoothened. Details for the final touches are carved in with a sharp knife. This procedure, which requires a high degree of accuracy, can only be achieved by skilled professional workmen. Followed by firing, each figurine is glazed and painted. The coloring is done with a delicate shading of dark and soft colors, rather than coloring with one color only. In some figurines, coloring is done by gradation. This is seen in the works of the dog and cat series, especially expressed in their hair and spots. The eyes, brows and lips of the faces of figures and animals are done by skilled workmen. After the painting is finished, the figurine pieces are glazed and finally fired. Usually, the temperature of the heat in which porcelain is fired is between 1,350 to 1,400 degrees celsius. Threfore, such porcelain statuettes are harder compared to the breakable tin-glazed earthen figures.

Flower baskets and lace

In the previous section, I have discussed the attractive features of Lladró porcelain statuettes. The diversity of motifs, the movements and expression of feelings of the figures and animals, gentle tone of color, surprisingly precise techniques – their total balance creates beautiful masterpieces.

This book concentrates on the Lladró flower basket series, heads of beautiful women with lace, and lace ballet shoes as objects. They directly enhance the gentlesness, delicateness and gracefulness of the pieces. Besides the porcelain of practical use, the flower basket was the first small piece that Lladró made. Ornaments with bouquets and flowers in them were made first during the Renaissance in Italy by Luca della Robbia and the majolica potters. The traditional strings spread throughout Europe and were manufactured in many porcelain factories. However, as previously mentioned, the petals of flowers of majolica and other tin-glazed clay flowers are slightly thicker to avoid cracks when firing. After the mid-18th century, when porcelain spread to Europe, there was no difference between tin-glazed clay flowers and flower baskets and those of porcelain. Compared to other flowers and flower baskets, those of Lladró had thin petals, whose fibers are carved in a relief. This seems simple; however, patience and dexterity of a skilled and experienced craftsman is highly demanded to shape the petals. Some twenty to thirty petals, of sizes large and small, are shaped by hand one by one. Then the petals are combined like those of real flowers, followed by adding of leaves. As shaping is done, flowers are gathered together and tied with a ribbon or placed in a basket. This is a very complicated process.

The flower baskets mentioned here are wrapped in lace. This enhances the prettiness of the flowers. The use of lace is another characteristic of Lladró's art. The bust of a woman wrapped in lace, lace flower baskets, lace ballet shoes –they are gentle, pure, elegant, as well as graceful.

Lace expresses gentleness, purity, elegance and grace. In the 17th and 18th centuries, lace was not only used for outfits of women, but also those for men and children of aristocrats as well as for folk costumes.

Purity is expressed in the porcelain pieces of woman wrapped in white and black veils. She may be a virgin who went to a mass at church. Such expression is made possible only with porcelain, and not with marble or clay. Lace for porcelain had been used in 18th-century statuettes by Kandler of Meissen and by craftsmen of Chelsea. Such porcelain pieces as the woman's bust, flower baskets, and ballet shoes emphasize the beauty of lace, but the technique is complex. After shape made as desired, coloring, glazing, and removing the excess paint from the holes of the lace, and firing again. It the lace is not adhered well enough to the clay, the lace might break. If the dip is too thick, the holes of the lace will get stuffed; if too

*Collection of teaspoons. Colors of each of the handles
are different. On the ends of the design of leaves,
the logo of Lladró is drawn. On the top of the spoon,
there is a relief of a basket with three roses.*

Lace baskets filled with bouvardias. These baskets seem like they were sent from nymphs from a flower garden. In each of the three different baskets, there are different flowers. Lladró has over 5.000 color samples; here the colors are pastels, which create gracefulness in their color matching.

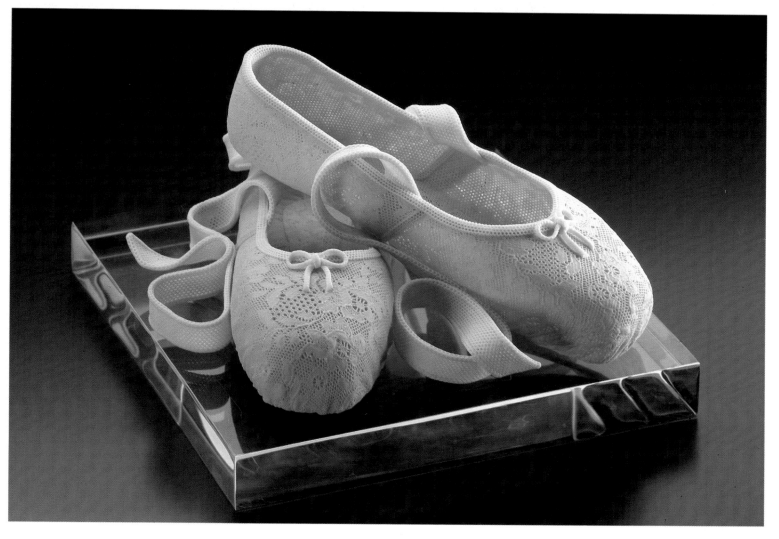

Among Lladró porcelains there is one that faithfully reproduces ballet shoes. Placed in a casual way, we can imagine that the ballerina wearing them has just finished her performance.

One of the characteristics of feminine figures in Lladró porcelain is that the qualities of gentleness and purity are expressed through the use of a painstaking technique. The woman's white skin is like a relief under the black lace, enhancing her modesty. Could she be a young Spanish woman in church? The lace over her head seems to be truly real.

Here we have the same woman's bust as on the previous page. In this case, however, it was more difficult to express her feelings since the piece is in white porcelain. Great skill was required on the part of the artist to distinguish the woman's complexion from the tone of the veil, since they are of the same colour. The contrast between the short fringe, the woman's forehead and the veil that casts a slight shadow endows the figure with vitality and gentleness.

The representation of lace here reaches the heights of complication since it is included in a basket of flowers.

thin, the dip might wash off. It is important to pay attention to the amount of water.

The porcelain art of contemporary Spanish artist Lladró has thus been discussed. About fifteen years ago, I found a small statue with soft colors of an angel at a store in a hotel in Madrid. Their cute expressions and movements caught my eyes; therefore, I bought two of them and added them to my collection. Since then, I have become interested in Lladró. Porcelain pieces of Meissen and Royal Copenhagen were already imported in Japan, but I could not yet find any of Lladró's at that time. In 1983, when Lladró's statuettes appeared in the Japanese market for the first time, their popularity has increased. People live to seek beautiful things, and Lladró porcelain attracts people with its pretty and gentle expressions. To me Lladró's small porcelain pieces are what Mozart's small musical pieces are to Beethoven's symphonies.

Another example of the highly delicate creations of Lladró porcelain are these fragile hats, an alternative sample of the pieces with lace.

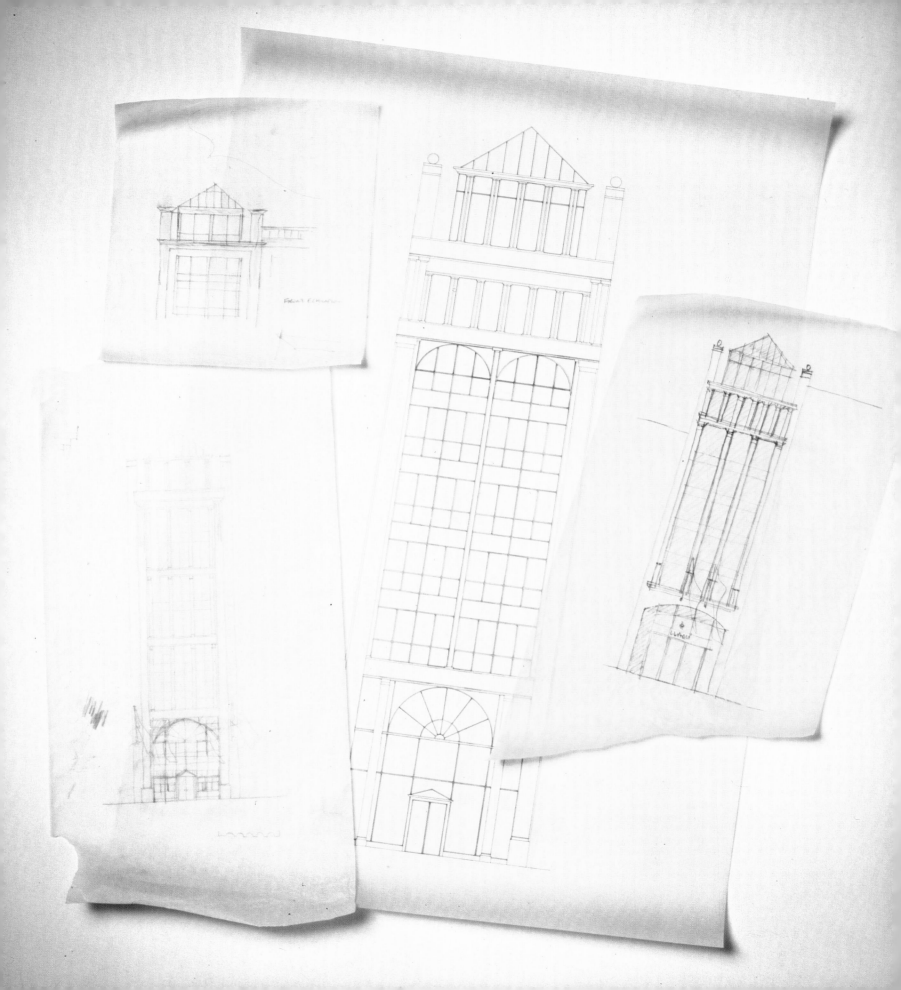

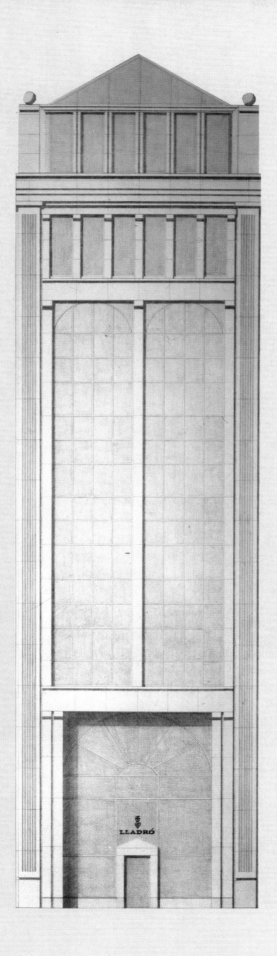

On this page and the opposite are the study drawings for the Lladró Museum on 57th Street, New York headquarters of the Lladró Collectors Society and the venue for a host of future cultural activities.

Left: the badge identifying members of the Lladró Collectors Society, with the signatures of its founders. Above: Hard cover of "Expressions"; this magazine gives detailed information about any novelties in the world of Lladró.

LLADRÓ COLLECTORS SOCIETY

Many years have gone by since the first Lladró porcelain workshop was set up at the beginning of the fifties. Almost forty years... This has been sufficient time —as the very passing of time itself has proved— for Lladró porcelain to gain a firm, permanent foothold in both the national and international markets and above all, to become highly esteemed by lovers of fine porcelain. No one could possibly deny this today. On the other hand, seen from another point of view this time has not been sufficient for it to be impossible to retrace one's steps a little in an attempt to recover and rescue from oblivion those first works created by the Lladró brothers at the beginning of their artistic career, works which might be lost forever with the passing of more time.

Now, at the present juncture where we find ourselves straddling two periods, one of complete and fecund artistic maturity and the other of new, wider artistic ventures, is the ideal moment to acquire, if one has not already done so, those aforementioned pieces that belong to the early days of Lladró production. The collector now has a unique opportunity to improve or complete his collection.

Furthermore, these first pieces —for the most part unable to be reproduced— in a few years' time will become far more valuable than they are now. As an example of this, suffice it to say that an early Lladró vase which fetched 7 dollars when it was originally sold is now valued at over 10,000 dollars. And all these early pieces will continue to increase steadily in value, becoming highly sought-after by collectors. For collectors, genuine

Example of the identity card of the Lladró Collectors Society.

collectors that is, are aware of the value of a work of art and that this value increases with the passing of time. Similarly, they recognise those works that will last and maintain unblemished the unalterable value of their aesthetic qualities. These people, who already possess the precious gift of being able to recognise, appreciate and love beauty, now have an added advantage in that the Lladró brothers have decided to make their search easier and offer the opportunity for greater security in their selection.

This was one of the reasons why the Lladró company set up the Lladró Collectors Society, a brand new association which, besides increasing the firm's prestige, informs regular customers and porcelain lovers in general about any developments affecting porcelain production or concerning the

needs and desires of the potential buyer. Every collector of these porcelain pieces and any person interested in them can be a member of the society. All members are given a member's card and, as such, they are entitled to receive certain gifts and to acquire advantageously special figures that Lladró creates exclusively for them once a year and which, evidently, will also finally be of considerable value. Indeed, one of these pieces two years after its creation has reached a market value ten times greater than its original one. These special figures so far created are the ones entitled *Payasito con Perritos* (Boy-clown with Puppies), which appeared in 1985 and to which we have just referred, *Payasito Contemplativo* (Thoughtful Boy-clown), dated 1986 and *Ramos de Primavera* (Spring Bouquets), dated 1987.

The best that Lladró can put into the representation of little boys is clearly reflected in this last piece. The childlike expression is perfect in its innocence, while the reproduction of the flower bouquets is a veritable tour de force. There is such a variety of flowers and they are so accurately reproduced that one can almost smell their fragrance. Each flower was lovingly and painstakingly made by hand, petal by petal, by an undisputed master in this difficult art. This is the figure produced for collectors in 1987 and which can be acquired by them until April 1988.

An important facet of the wide range of activities of the Lladró Collectors Society is the setting up of the Lladró Museum, housed in its own building on 57th Street, between Fifth and Sixth Avenues, in New York. This museum is due to be opened a few months from the time of going to print.

The work of the architects Rafael Tamarit and Carlos Brillembourg, the museum premises, with its elegant glass entrance, will contribute yet another note of elegance in 57th Street, where there is already an abundance of fine establishments. This exquisite "wrapping" will, however, house an even more valuable content, since this fine, original building will be, above all, a meeting place for those who enjoy and appreciate porcelain, and a venue where all can exchange information. Similarly, it will be the permanent setting for a great variety of cultural and artistic events and activities. For example, occupying two whole floors there will be permanent exhibitions of Lladró porcelain, from exceptional works, such as the sculptures used for

the first pieces and those pertaining to limited editions now withdrawn, to a highly unusual collection of decorated vases and bowls. On another floor there will be an exhibition of contemporary works which will succeed each other in a constant turnover of different series.

It is planned also to show daily films in the museum amphitheatre, films in which visitors can become familiar with the activities in the Lladró workshops in Spain and which will moreover introduce them to the members of the Lladró family. Occasionally in the same amphitheatre talks will be given and demostrations made, all to the benefit of Lladró collectors.

Along these same lines and within the framework of the activities of the Lladró Collectors Society, a number of tours have been organised from the United States for members of the society, offering them the marvellous opportunity of visiting a number of Spanish cities, each one with its own particular interest, during 1988 and at different times and following different itineraries. As well as that of visiting the city of Lladró porcelain, during which they will be able to see first hand the whole manufacturing process.

A California jeweller, Herb Rostand, is closely linked to the world of our collectors, being considered the pioneer of the "secondary market" of Lladró. When at a certain moment there was a serious crisis in the jewellery business, due to the sudden increase in the price of gold and precious stones, Rostand decided, in view of the circumstances, to expand the horizons of his business and set it in a new direction. It was thus that, in his search for new resources and elements

*Above, **one of the pieces produced for the Lladró Collectors Society depicting*** *the most human world of clowns.*

with which to revive his business, he came across Lladró porcelain, which immediately attracted all his admiration and attention and became the new stage in his professional activity. From that moment onwards Rostand began to seek out and buy as many Lladró figures as he could find and fill his workshops with them. This was how the so-called "secondary market" of Lladró came into being, to which collectors began to repair increasing numbers in search of figures that could no longer be found on the market. The house of Rostand thus offered collectors the opportunity to buy —and occasionally sell— pieces that otherwise they would have no hope of acquiring. For this reason, Rostand's challenge now is to actually find these now irreplaceable pieces to be able to offer them to the ever increasing demand on the part of collectors.

In 1987, and not only for members of the Lladró Collectors Society, Lladró presented a special Christmas piece, for the first time in the history of the company. It consists of a handmade porcelain bell, destined to become one of the most valuable collectors' pieces. The work, which does not depart from the Lladró tradition, is finely decorated in bas-relief and shows two groups of carol singers enveloped in snowflakes that fall from above. On the matt surface of this bell the year of issue has been engraved, a detail that raises even more the value of the piece.

On the other hand, Lladró is preparing the Collectors' Catalogue, a complete sample of photographs of all the porcelain figures created by Lladró since their beginnings in the fifties. This catalogue, which includes brief information on

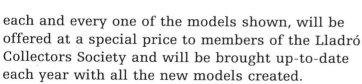

Lladró identity mark on one of the pieces showing, furthermore, that the work is exclusively for members of the Society.

each and every one of the models shown, will be offered at a special price to members of the Lladró Collectors Society and will be brought up-to-date each year with all the new models created.

With a view to keeping alive at all times relations with the public, the Lladró Collectors Society publishes a three-monthly magazine called "Expressions" which members receive free. This magazine, which at the moment is published only in English, given the considerable membership the Society has managed to gather in North America,

gives detailed information about any novelties in the world of Lladró, such as the launching of new models or the definitive withdrawal of others from the market.

Similarly, and with the same end in view, special receptions, meetings and exhibitions have been arranged in which collectors meet from a host of different places and take advantage of the opportunity to see, know and buy new pieces and, above all, to exchange impressions about a subject that fascinates them. Some of these receptions,

such as the one organised by Douglas Lorie in his Worth Avenue galleries, Palm Beach, Florida, have been attended by members of the Lladró family, who took the opportunity to put their signatures on many of the pieces the guests acquired during the function.

Perhaps one of the most interesting of these exchanges of impressions and information we have mentioned is the one referring to the extent and content of the different collections of members and to the way in which they entered the world of Lladró porcelain. Equally interesting is the way in which these members plan to increase their collections, especially in the cases where a collector regrets not being able to find a specific figure which he has seen in a catalogue or in a

This little girl with flowers is an interesting example of the delicacy of the *colouring. The figure is also for the Lladró Collectors Society.*

friend's house but which he has been unable to find in any establishment. In these cases, such figures must be ordered specially from an authorised Lladró retailer.

Thus the Lladró Collectors Society has opened a wide, promising gate to collectors in search of rare pieces, both those who began their collection at the beginning of Lladró's career and those who began it later. Finally, it can be said that the Lladró Collectors Society has made it possible, after almost forty years, for collectors to begin or complete their collections of these exceptional, exquisite porcelain pieces which, without absolutely any room for doubt, have become truly classical works of contemporary art.

This exquisite girl, with her sumptuous clothes, her case and her bouquet of flowers, has been voted the Lladró Collectors Society piece for 1988

EXPRESSIONS
MAGAZINE

LLADRÓ COLLECTORS SOCIETY

Vol. 1, No. 1, SPRING 1985 $3.00

EXPRESSIONS
MAGAZINE

LLADRÓ COLLECTORS SOCIETY

Vol. 1, No. 2, SUMMER 1985 $3.00

The first Lladró office building was modest in comparison to the multi-building factory complex currently occupied by the company. At the time it was built, however, it was a long awaited and impressive tribute to the success of the enterprise.

lowed, including a violinist, a ballet dancer and a Harlequin-Columbine couple. What soon came to market were porcelains addressing a vast repertoire of subjects and themes—from those inspired by Chinese history and sculpture to others interpreting literary and social subjects.

The capabilities and enthusiasms of the guiding forces at Lladró were continually translated into porcelains with an ever-growing international following. An export program was initiated when the first factory opened, and

the market outside of Spain blossomed immediately. In addition, the 60s decade brought Lladró to the attention of a notable collection of celebrities who made visits to the Lladró factory or its exhibitions. Among the personalities that came to admire Lladró's achievements were the Swedish Ambassador to Spain (1964), the then Prince and Princess of Spain, Don Juan Carlos de Bourbon and Doña Sofía (1966), Manuel Gonzalez Marti, the founder of the National Museum of Ceramics in Valencia (1969) and the U.S. Consul and U.S. Ambassador to Spain (1969).

The interest in Lladró, from kings and queens to ordinary citizens, was evident early on. This reception of truly royal proportions further sparked the creative energies and aggressive marketing posture of the now well-equipped Lladró company. And under the tutelage of its determined and talented founders, the genesis of Lladró, from tiny workshop to internationally renowned resource, was completed.

14

The treasures of Valencia are many and include the 18th century Church of Santa Catalina with its graceful baroque belfry. Beyond the city limits (facing page, top to bottom) one finds lush orange groves and, along the Mediterranean, sandy beaches and calm waters. Another Valencian reminder of the past are the Towers of Serranos. Built by Pere Balaguer in 1398 as a gateway in the town walls, they combine the splendor of a triumphal arch with the sturdiness of a bastion.

On these two pages there are selections from "Expressions Magazine", the journal given free to members of the Lladró Collectors Society, containing information of particular interest to them.

Exclusively for MEMBERS

Introducing... Little Pals... our very first figurine made for members only. This disarming figurine is very special to those of us at the Lladró Collectors Society and we hope that it comes to mean as much to those of you who will be eligible to collect Little Pals when it becomes available this Fall.

The designing of a figurine that would be made available only to those who became members of the Lladró Collectors Society during 1985 was a true labor of love for everyone involved. Because this figurine is our way of saying thank you for being such avid Lladró admirers and collectors and dedicated supporters of our Society, we wanted it to embody many of those characteristics that first attracted you to Lladró and continues to do so. We also wanted this members-only figurine to be distinctive, to serve as a reminder to those who own it that Little Pals was made for a select few of our collectors and would not be available to the general public. (continued on next page)

...ad with Lladró

...information with them ...ed it would be... interest... ...nd we look forward with ...more Lladró gatherings in □

Lladró admirers selected figurines for autographing by Señor Lladró at Stowell's, Natick, Mass. (top left). A special customer and the owners of Tender Thoughts stole a rare quiet moment with Señor and Señora Lladró (bottom left), while shoppers at Wanamaker's, Philadelphia, viewed a video about Lladró.

Society Appoints Assistant Director

It's been only six months since we introduced the Lladró Collectors Society and we're happy to report that the responses have

Collectors Society, and invitations to attend special events made it clear that our staff had to be expanded. Therefore, we recently welcomed Susan Stashkevetch to the Lladró Collectors Society as the assistant director.

In her capacity as the assistant director of the Society, Ms. Stashkevetch will handle all public relations projects, including the scheduling of special events. She will be responsible for the Society's member and chapter programs and will serve as the editor of Expressions,

personal appearances and interviews. No stranger to the world of porcelain art, she comes to the Society from Gifts & Decorative Accessories magazine where she was the managing editor.

If you find that you have any questions concerning the Collectors Society or the Lladró figurines you own, Ms. Stashkevetch will see that your inquiries are answered. And her face is sure to become a familiar one as she travels around the country meeting with those of you who collect or

LLADRÓ: THE RITES OF PASSAGE

Three brothers—three different, yet compatible resources—were all pulling in the same direction to help transform a fledgling firm into a respectable, flourishing porcelain-making business. That was the scenario in 1953 when the Lladró company, still located at the elder Lladró's Almacera home, was officially founded. In the short period of two years Juan, José and Vicente had found it necessary to expand the labor force to 28 workers, a remarkable achievement considering that the post World War II years were less than fertile

ones for a growing young business dedicated to an endeavor like the manufacture of porcelain decoratives. However, the three brothers challenged and indeed beat the odds and were now on the road to expansion.

The start-up phase ended in 1955 when an outlet store was opened in Valencia. It was the beginning of the end of economic difficulties for Lladró and a move that demanded the transition from tiny family workshop to factory. The retail shop and the demands it brought forced the brothers to

become businessmen as well as artists. In the name of industry and progress they laid the foundation for their first factory, in the neighboring town of Tabernes Blanques, in 1958.

During this period, the Lladró brothers began to gather new collaborators, workers and assistants for their operations. The brothers organized highly specialized departments and laboratories, which attracted teams of porcelain artists with the best experience. And as the growth needs of the staff continued to expand, a vocational training school was inaugurated on Dec. 22, 1963. During this time the board of directors was also enlarged to include five members.

The international develop-

Gifts of Lladró have become an artistic signature for the Lladró studios. Here, The Hunters exemplifies this style.

Gifts of Lladró have been received by numerous statesmen, religious leaders, and royalty throughout the years. Among them was Pope Paul VI, who was given a set of Lladró's Three Wise Men. When the Pontiff met Neil Armstrong, Edwin Aldrin, and Michael Collins, the first Americans to visit the moon, he presented each astronaut with one of the figures. On this occasion, Pope Paul made a comparison between the Wise Men—messengers of God—and the astronauts—messengers in space. When the three Lladró brothers learned of the Pope's gift, they presented His Holiness with another set.

The two color catalogs of yesteryear are in strong contrast to the full-color publications of today's Lladró.

ment boom of the 1960s extended to Lladró where the grand tradition of European porcelain was being abandoned and a return to earlier themes, such as vessels made with bucaro clay and flowers, was pursued with great vigor. The competitive prices and quality of materials and craftsmanship, already Lladró standards, were fused with a distinctive design—elongated figures reminiscent of the iconography of El Greco. Used in tandem with a palette of more than 5,000 shades, including blue, cream, grey and pale brown, a Lladró "look" was created.

By 1965, the now famous Harlequin had been marketed with great success, reinforcing the emerging Lladró image. A small collection of stylized figures fol-
(continued on next page)

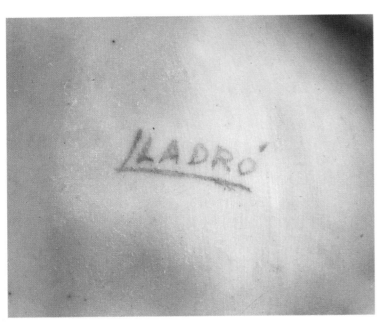

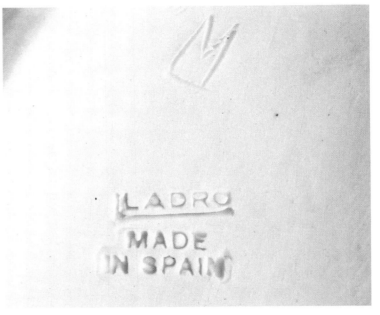

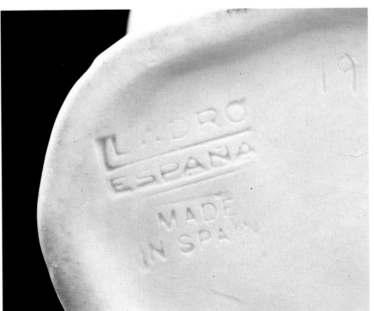

Identity marks

The best mark that a work of art can display is the imprint of the personality that created it. This is especially true in the case of works in which the hand of man had a direct part to play, such as in ceramics.

Ceramics is an art that man began to practice at the dawn of his existence. This man used his hands only with which to model the clay and his incipient creative capacity passed integrally to them from his mind. Thus in those rough creations the personal stamp of the craftsman began to emerge, each man's individual way of doing things.

With the passing of centuries, this primitive individual production of exclusively domestic use became more ornamental and collective. In classical Greece there were many ceramic workshops in operation —ceramics that were painted and which, for identification purposes, were "signed". It is well known that soon these creations began to spread over the Mediterranean. The same happened in ancient Rome, which imitated, assimilated and adopted many Greek techniques in the manufacture of ceramics and also printed its own stamp which we can still see today perfectly engraved on the bottoms of vessels and plates. Precisely for this reason, this type of ceramics was called *sigillata.*

Thus, each one with its own particular characteristics and following paths which were sometimes parallel and sometimes divergent, the ceramics of each country, each region and each manufacture became increasingly personalised until, in the mid XVIIIth century, Europe discovered porcelain.

With this new, superior quality material it became possible to produce pieces of much greater value, and the need for identifying marks now became even more inevitable. This was not because porcelain works all had the same characteristics, since any amateur with a good eye could distinguish between them, but because porcelain manufacture had become the mean to satisfy a refined, cultured society that requested luxury items of quality which were also genuine. This became the tonic from then on.

Today the firm of Lladró porcelain has adopted the same practice of engraving its identifying marks on all the pieces in its collection. In the first years this was not considered necessary since Lladró porcelain has such an original form that in can be identified with the utmost ease; Lladró pieces have that personal stamp that most distinguishes the work of one artist from that of another, the production of an artistic school from that of another. However, the moment came when it *was* considered necessary, for in every creative process the point is reached where the artist feels the need to secure and confirm his work, to make it more his own with this kind of certificate of realization, to guarantee that what the collector is holding in his hands and contemplating is not just any work but *his* work, the work that he, the artist, has created.

The Lladró identifying marks are now the guarantee of authenticity of each of the pieces; they are like the signature of the artists who have created them. And we say marks in the plural since a variety of different ones are used all of which, needless to say, have the same validity. Even when, as in the case of one of these marks —prior to 1974— a spelling mistake slips in to be preserved, perhaps forever, on a delicate feminine figure or on the agile body of an animal. These orthographical errors not only do not lessen the value or the worth of the figure but, on the contrary, give it a new dimension as a rarity much sought after by those collectors who have a love of the unusual.

Just as the flag that flies on the main mast of a ship tells the open sea to which country she belongs, so the Lladró identity marks inform the collector of the age of the piece or, if it has just been acquired, tell him that it belongs, without any doubt, to the wonderful "country" of Lladró porcelain.

A reproduction of some of the marks by means of which to identify Lladró porcelain.

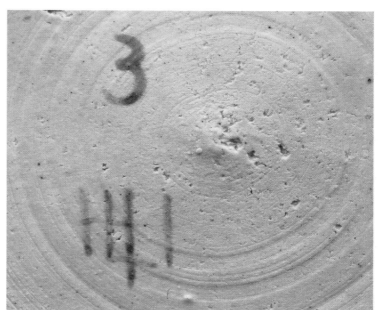

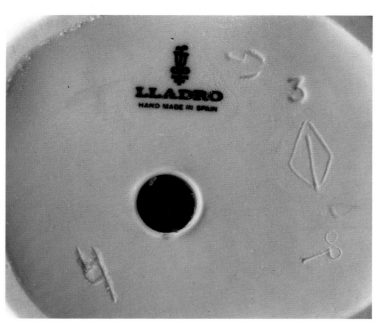